First published 2016 by Focal Press
70 Blanchard Road, Suite 402, Burlington, MA 01803

and by Focal Press
711 Third Avenue, New York, NY 10017, USA
2 Park Square, Milton Park, Abingdon, Oxon OX14 4RN

First issued in hardback 2017

Focal Press is an imprint of the Taylor & Francis Group, an informa business

Library of Congress Cataloging in Publication Data
Sullivan, Brian, 1965-
The design studio method : creative problem solving with UX sketching / by Brian
Sullivan ; illustrated by J. Schuh.
pages cm
ISBN 978-1-138-02256-0 (pbk.) -- ISBN 978-1-315-77702-3 (ebk.) 1. Web sites--Design--
Technique. 2. User-centered system design. 3. Research teams. 4. Storyboards. I. Title.
TK5105.888.S79 2015
006.7'8--dc23
2014039138

Typeset in Myriad Pro and Avenir by
Servis Filmsetting Ltd, Stockport, Cheshire

ISBN 13: 978-1-1380-2256-0 (pbk)
ISBN 13: 978-1-1384-7539-7 (hbk)

Table of Contents

Bound to Create

You are a creator.

Whatever your form of expression — photography, filmmaking, animation, games, audio, media communication, web design, or theatre — you simply want to create without limitation. Bound by nothing except your own creativity and determination.

Focal Press can help.

For over 75 years Focal has published books that support your creative goals. Our founder, Andor Kraszna-Krausz, established Focal in 1938 so you could have access to leading-edge expert knowledge, techniques, and tools that allow you to create without constraint. We strive to create exceptional, engaging, and practical content that helps you master your passion.

Focal Press and you.

Bound to create.

Focal Press
Taylor & Francis Group

Acknowledgements

I would like to thank my wife, Susan Sullivan, for her unwavering support. As always, she was patient through my writing and revisions. At dinner, my wife and I would talk about the book with our son, Sean Sullivan. If you want some sharp perspective, share your thoughts with a smart, 15-year-old teenager.

Next, I want to thank Anita Cator. When I decided to do my first design studio project, Anita immediately stepped up to the challenge. Anita and her design team (Ryan Merritt, Sam Oh, Kimberly Richards, Trey Pace, Cason Swindle) would offer many suggestions to improve the overall process. Anita and I have spent hundreds of hours planning, organizing, executing, and perfecting the methods presented in this book. Anita is a first-rate designer and thought leader.

I want to thank my mom (Edith Sullivan), brother (Kevin Sullivan), oldest sister (Sharon Davis), and sibling rival/sister (Lisa Bell). My step-children (Laura Martinez and Joseph Vatalaro) have made me proud. Thanks to Laura's husband, Frank Martinez, for late-night laughs and iced tea. My big, fat Irish family includes: Steve, Kim, Paul, Cassidy, Tanner, Kaylee, Connor, Tim, Alan, Brad, Austin, Tammie, Tyler, and Alyssa. I am blessed to have support from each of you.

I love you, Mom! I miss Dad every day!

A special thanks goes to my co-workers—Anna Harasimiuk and Kris Courtney. You have taught me many lessons about design, usability, business, project management, and life. It has been my pleasure (and honor) to have worked with you for almost 10 years.

J. Schuh has been a wonderful co-conspirator on the creation of this book. I have enjoyed our conversations and his illustrations. We did encounter a happy accident with one illustration. One of my original sketches was misinterpreted by J. Schuh into a completely different concept. His drawing was too good to dismiss—a happy accident! This illustration forced me to rethink and rewrite an entire section of the book. With my words and his illustrations, you get a "Sullivan-Schuh One-Two" reading experience. He was challenging some ideas, while cheerleading other ones.

For me, partnership starts with J.

The reviewers of the book gave so much advice and time. Thank you— Preston McCauley, Marti Gold, Aaron Irrizary, Marc Gilpin, Anita Cator,

Nathan Shedroff, J. Schuh, and Susan Sullivan. Aaron Irrizary's comments forced me to restructure six chapters. Marti Gold's comments moved entire sections around the whole book. When I first saw the comments in red ink from Susan Sullivan, I thought someone had bled on my second draft.

It takes a tribe to write a book. You will always be my tribe.

A very, very special thanks to the Big Design Conference team: Keith Anderson, Lara Becker, Jeremy Johnson, Candy Bernhardt, Fred Janis, Lorie Whitaker, Joshua Winegardner, Adam Polansky, J. Schuh, and A.J. Wood. We put on a great design conference each year. I am inspired by each of you!

Special words of encouragement were greatly appreciated during some late nights of writing: Mitch Todd, Lissa Duty, John Nossal, Molly Holschlag, Tony Cecala, Brenda Huettner, Adam Connor, Elizabeth Rosenzweig, Russ Unger, Dana Chisnell, Joshua Hall, Stephanie Brisendine, Cassini Nassir, Eva Warren, Ken Tabor, and many others. I am such a Mitch Todd fan.

Lastly, I want to thank two people at Focal Press: David Bevans and Mary LaMacchia. David, you believed in me. Mary, you guided me through the production process. Your enthusiasm for the project was contagious.

I am so stoked! Enjoy.

Introduction

Welcome to the first edition of *The Design Studio Method* book. Design studios are sketching workshops, where key stakeholders produce sketches individually and critique them with a group. On the surface, design studios appear to be simple to do: sketch and critique.

The single best thing you can do at the start of a project is a design studio.

Yet, most people do not run very effective design studios. Over the past 10 years, I was appalled to see the lack of structure and focus in design studios. Participants would argue, compete for attention, ignore other opinions, and so on. Leaders did not seem to grasp the importance of providing simple rules to help people focus, thinking tools to help people envision different perspectives, and ways to more effectively work with remote people and get executive support.

So, I decided to write this book.

How to Use This Book

Painters love and hate blank canvases. Writers love and hate the blank page. Designers love and hate the emptiness of white space. This love–hate relationship with empty white things (canvases, pages, or screens) seems to be a natural balancing act for creative people. They love the design freedom of an empty space and hate the white void that needs to be filled. For many designers, the act of designing defines them. The finished work may not be as fulfilling as the act of creation.

Design studios offer a collaborative method for designers and other professionals to co-create apps, workflows, and sites. Many creative professionals prefer to work in silence and solitude. The act of making something pixel perfect requires concentration and precision. Noisy neighbors are not welcomed.

A mental space is needed to think, experiment, re-think, calibrate, re-do, and design.

Yet, digital designers need ways to successfully collaborate with other humans. Technical solutions move beyond the realm of the lone designer

"It's so fine and yet so terrible to stand in front of a blank canvas."
– Paul Cézanne

sitting in an ivory tower, hoping for inspiration. For these designers, the act of creation requires communication, cooperation, and collaboration. Other professionals can turn their mockups into a digital reality. The best tool to help web and app designers is a design studio.

I wrote *The Design Studio Method* to be used as a reference book.

When you first read this book, I recommend that you read it from start to finish. In the early chapters, I go over several key concepts that get repeated throughout the book. By reading the entire book, you get a holistic view of the design studio method. It is complete with rules and tools to help you structure your next design studio projects.

As you perform your first project, I recommend you review the Summary section at the end of each chapter. Each summary provides a high-level review of the chapter. You may want to review a section from a particular chapter in greater detail. The summaries should help you to plan and execute your next design studio.

You may want to read only the real-world example within each chapter. The example helps you to see the implementation of the various steps of a design studio. You might find some hidden insights in the example, after you have performed your own design studios.

I encourage you to fine-tune the concepts you read in this book.

If you want to get somewhere, you need a GPS connection. This book is meant to serve as a road map for doing more effective collaboration when you use the design studio method. Use this book as a reference guide for your future endeavors.

PART 1

Processes

CHAPTER 1

Book Overview

The design studio method has been used by art colleges, boutique design companies, consultants, and advertising agencies for decades. In these settings, design professionals or students present their concepts and hear critiques of their work by their peers. In the last few years, Web Designers have started to use the design studio method with stakeholders to help the entire product team to generate and evaluate ideas before any software development begins.

"Creative problem solving is looking at the same thing as everyone else and thinking something different."
– Albert Szent-Gyorgi, Nobel Prize Winner

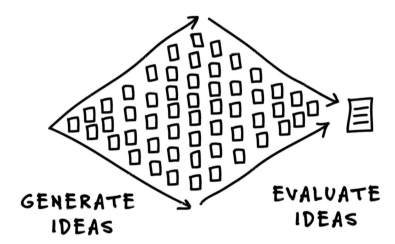

GENERATE IDEAS

EVALUATE IDEAS

While most business professionals do not have a formal design education, they do think visually. Marketers brainstorm new ideas on whiteboards. Developers sketch out data flows. User Experience Designers create mind maps, sketch mockups, and draw customer task flows. Database Administrators sketch entity relationship diagrams. **In short, truly creative solutions to problems often begin with some form of sketching.**

The purpose of this book is to help you understand how to harness the power of visual thinking at all levels of your organization by effectively using the design studio method in a business setting. The concepts described in this book are based upon well-established creative problem-solving research, which has been in use since the 1950s, by Alex Osborn, Sidney Parnes, Edward de Bono, Donald Treffinger, and Ruth Noller. In the first part of the book, you

*At its core, the design studio process is
simple:*

1. *People generate ideas by sketching their
   concepts.*
2. *A group comes together to show and
   critique other people's sketches.*
3. *Based upon the group's feedback,
   concepts get further refined.*

will learn how to apply these research-based principles to run an effective
design studio.

Advantages of Design Studios

Design studios provide a creative problem-solving method, where Designers,
Developers, and key stakeholders create and explore design alternatives.
Based upon my experience, the design studio method offers these
advantages:

- **Design studios are fast.** In most cases, design studios can be done in
  a few hours or days. This method is ideal for aggressive deadlines. Plus,
  design studios fit nicely into rapid development processes, such as Agile,
  Scrum, or Extreme Programming.
- **Design studios help you to visualize complex problems more easily.**
  You can more easily see relationships and make associations in a design
  studio than by reading a document or listening to another person. You
  visually see problems and solutions.
- **Design studios allow you to share knowledge.** You should include
  a cross-functional team of people with different backgrounds and
  experiences. Concepts get discussed from multiple viewpoints, which
  enrich and strengthen the final design.
- **Design studios promote team cohesiveness.** By spending time together,
  participants create a shared vision for the final design. Their commitment
  will be based upon their effort spent creating and evaluating the different
  concepts. Broken teams can heal.
- **Design studios help you to get early commitment on design
  direction.** When a design studio ends, the project team should know its
  design direction. As you move to production, the design will continue to
  be refined, but the design direction should be set.
- **Design studios can help you overcome communication barriers.**
  Participants must illustrate their ideas in a design studio. Since sketches
  will contain universal symbols of lines, circles, squares, and words, you can
  more easily overcome language barriers.

Where Do Design Studios Fit into a Product Workflow?

Every Designer uses sketching as a primary activity. Designers will sketch
notes, user personas, workflows, user interface elements, navigation options,
and more. Designers are very comfortable with sketching. The design studio
method fits nicely into their natural workflow.

The following illustration shows the typical artifacts of a web designer.

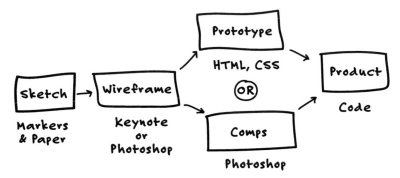

A Web Designer starts with sketching. When they have a design direction, some Designers will build a wireframe to help with requirements gathering. Customers provide feedback on the wireframes. The Designer will either build a set of comps or a prototype. Usability testing can be done on the prototype or comps. In the end, development will create the code to turn either the prototype or comps into production-ready code.

While the above workflow is a standard process for Designers, it can be foreign or intimidating to other professionals. Product Managers, Developers, Marketers, and other key stakeholders may see sketching as an activity they do periodically. They may not understand how it is an essential first step in the design process.

For some people, the very act of presenting their ideas in sketch form will be new and different. It will be exciting to some, daunting to others, and terrifying to a few people.

Nonetheless, over the past 10 years, I continue to hear participants tell me how much they enjoy the collaborative aspects of the design studio method. Often for the first time, the entire product team works together performing many group-related activities to create and clearly define new products. These include:

• Listening to people present their sketches.

• Asking and answering questions to clarify their sketches.

• Grouping together similar-looking sketches.

• Naming a group category with the other participants.

• Evaluating the positive and negative aspects of the various sketches.

• Voting on the most promising sketches.

• Re-sketching new ideas based on lessons learned in the design studio.

• Mashing up two different sketches on a whiteboard.

• Making decisions together to create a common vision.

After you have finished a design studio, your product team will have a strong sense of purpose and a common vision. Each member will be able to clearly and enthusiastically communicate that vision to their respective teams and stakeholders. This will result in faster development times, smarter decisions on features, and far better user experiences.

Design Studios Maximize Your Design Freedom

Design studios supercharge your design efforts by maximizing your design freedom at the start of a project. Designers use four types of design artifacts, or documents:

- **Sketches.** Designers use freehand sketches to visually think about a problem or a potential solution. These drawings do not represent the finished work.

- **Wireframes.** A wireframe is a visual representation of how a page or screen might appear to a customer. Designers use wireframes to flesh out the details of a design.

- **Prototypes.** A prototype is a simulation of a product (or feature) to evaluate a design in a test environment. The prototype mimics what a customer may see in production.

- **Final Deliverables.** Final deliverables include page designs (or comps), cascading style sheets, front-end code, and more used by the site or app in a product release.

As shown below, these design artifacts get used at different stages of software development.

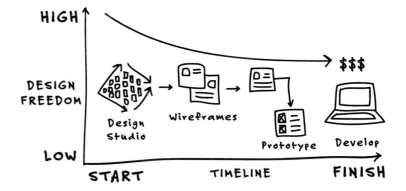

At the beginning of a project, your design freedom is very high. Developers have not started coding. Product Managers are trying to figure out customer requirements, timelines, and resource availability. Marketing messages and plans seem far away. During the early days of a project, Designers sketch many things—task flows, site maps, user stories, personas, storyboards, and design concepts. In most work settings, Designers will sketch alone. From time to time, you will see Designers collaborate by sketching together on a whiteboard.

Sketching is a natural act for Designers, but it does not have to be a solitary one. Design studios provide a method for Designers to collaboratively sketch with their product team. Before any software code is written, you can maximize your design freedom in a design studio.

TIP #1:

The single best thing you can do at the start of any project is a design studio.

Design Studios Prevent Escalation of Commitment

As decisions get made on a project, a product team will get behind specific ideas to deliver to their customers. **Your design freedom decreases with each decision that gets made.**

When an initial direction is determined, Designers will be pressured by Product Managers, Marketers, Developers, and other stakeholders to move from sketching to production. People no longer want to see sketches. Instead, they want to see realistic depictions in a wireframe or interactive prototype. With each passing day, a natural **escalation of commitment** occurs.

TIP #2:

An escalation of commitment occurs when a person spends a lot of time on a specific idea. You begin to think you cannot be wrong.

As people spend more time on a common goal, they become more committed to it. In their minds, they truly believe they cannot be wrong. They have worked hard (and long) on this vision. Marketing plans, training guides, lines of code, and quality-assurance testing has been completed. Design gets squeezed between tight deadlines, highly competitive markets, and the steadfast march towards product delivery.

Design studios can prevent this escalation of commitment. Designers usually become aware of many product decisions after they have been made. Design studios offer a method for Designers to be included in gathering customer requirements, making decisions, and setting a strategic vision for the next product release. Designers do not have to fight against the current product direction; they can help to set the strategic path in a design studio.

Common Barriers to Overcome

While design studios are common in art schools and advertising, in the business world you may encounter barriers that you need to overcome. Some barriers are imposed from external sources, while others are self-inflicted. You may not be able to overcome all of the barriers, and in some cases, the barrier will become a design constraint. If you lead a design studio, you need to understand these barriers for yourself to help you interact with participants.

Barriers usually fall into two types: business and personal barriers.

Understanding Business Barriers

Business barriers are restrictions placed upon your design studio by your company or some other external force. New legislation, tax incentives, a court decision, or government oversight are examples of external business forces. Time, money, and resources are internal business forces that always impact business decisions. In a design studio, the mix of individuals, the location of participants, their availability, and manager buy-in are additional examples of company business barriers.

You have little control over business barriers, but they do help you to understand constraints of your design problem. For example, the federal government enacted the Wright Amendment in 1979 to govern traffic at Dallas Love Field. In its original form, airlines could only fly non-stop flights to destinations within Texas and its surrounding states. For airlines operating out of Love Field, this federal law was both a business barrier and a design constraint. Low prices, customer service, and on-time performance allowed Southwest Airlines to differentiate itself from its competitors, even with the external force of the Wright Amendment affecting its business.

Again, you have little control over business barriers.

Understanding Personal Barriers

While you have little control over business barriers, you may be able to influence a personal barrier from a design studio participant. Personal barriers prevent people from being creative. Let's review a few personal barriers and how you can overcome them.

- **"I am not creative."** This personal barrier may be used because of a lack of confidence or being out of practice. Innovation and creativity scholars tell us that everyone has the capacity to be creative. Plus, the design studio method gives you tools and techniques to be creative.

- **"Nobody will ever like my ideas."** When you first show an idea, you will usually get a negative reaction from people. In design studios, you use positive judgment first, and the final sketch will combine several design elements from several sketches.

- **"I do not want to be humiliated."** It is painful to have your ideas rejected. The design studio has built-in mechanisms to prevent humiliation. Critiques of sketches look at design intent and execution. Only two negative comments are allowed for each idea. Nobody should be humiliated in a design studio.

- **"I do not have time."** Everyone is busy. Design studios are fast. In most cases, the participants can be done in 4 hours. For example, I worked on a design studio for a small user interface element. Participants sketched over 50 ideas (42 initial sketches, 7 re-sketches, and 1 final sketch) in just 5 hours. Design studios are a great way to invest your time!

- **"What's in it for me?"** In this case, people want to know if a project is worth their time. When people ask this question, I tell them that the design studio method provides them with a powerful tool to influence the strategic direction of their product. Plus, they can be part of the future solution.

With the design studio method, a strong leader can overcome a person's fear of failure, feeling of futility, lack of confidence, and anxiety over humiliation.

> **PERSONAL BARRIER = MARKETING OPPORTUNITY**
>
> *When someone gives you a personal barrier, consider it a marketing opportunity to review all of the advantages of the design studio method—fun, interactive, fast, and a shared design direction. You will be surprised at how quickly they want to participate.*

No Artistic Skills Needed to Sketch

You do not have to be an artist to sketch. Sketching is about visual thinking. As shown below, I quickly sketched three different images for a cup of coffee. Below these sketches, J. Schuh, the illustrator of this book, rendered these sketches into illustrations on his computer.

In a design studio, sketching is about getting your ideas on paper for other people to critique. You do not have to be an artist to sketch.

TIP #3:

You do not have to be an artist to sketch.

SKETCHING IS NOT THE SAME AS DRAWING

Design Studios Require Creative and Critical Thinking

Design studios require creative and critical thinking as participants generate and evaluate sketched ideas. We can define creative and critical thinking in these ways in a design studio:

- **Creative Thinking.** Creative thinking involves generating ideas, using your intuition, embracing ambiguity, using your imagination, and searching for meaningful connections. In a design studio, creative thinking occurs when participants sketch, re-sketch, and mash up ideas.

- **Critical Thinking.** Critical thinking involves a careful and constructive evaluation of the sketches. In a design studio, participants will organize, analyze, rank, prioritize, and choose the most viable concepts to merge into a final sketch. Participants should critique sketches using positive judgment first.

Managing creative and critical thinking is the key to running an effective design studio.

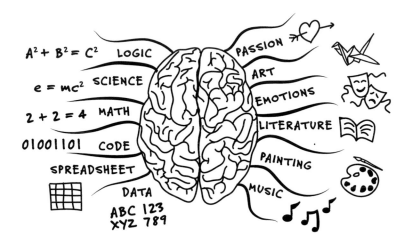

Most people believe creative and critical thinking are diametrically opposed. In your own work, you may believe people are either creative or critical thinkers. You might see a creative person as fun, approachable, eccentric, and friendly. On the other hand, you might see a critical thinker as intense, distant, analytical, and serious. Innovation and creativity scholars reveal that effective problem-solvers do both creative and critical thinking.

In my design studios, I use the metaphor of the left and right brain as a communication tool. According to myth, creative people are right-brained and critical people are left-brained. Innovation and creativity scholars dispel the myth of the left and right brain. In fact, the brain is a very complex organ. I use the myth of left-brain/right-brain as a communication tool to get people focused on the principles and processes of the design studio method.

Suggestions for Using This Book

For the first-time reader, you should read this book from cover to cover to get an initial understanding of the design studio method. The book is written in three parts:

- **Part 1: Processes.** These chapters provide you with the overall structure of design studios, processes to increase your productivity, and tools you can use with your participants to help them generate and evaluate ideas. You might consider these chapters as things you need to know before doing a design studio.

- **Part 2: Procedures.** These chapters provide you with step-by-step instructions that you can use when you perform a design studio. Within each chapter, you will find tips, best practices, stories, and a real-world example.

- **Part 3: Advanced Topics.** These chapters cover special topics, including saving your work, revisiting it, working remotely with people, and next steps.

Use the Summary section at the end of each chapter to help you recall key information.

When you perform your first design studio, keep this book handy and refer to the appropriate chapter. In addition, you may want to read the story behind the real-world example of the World Usability Day widget to get a better understanding of what you need to do. Finally, the book has a companion website, where you can find additional information including videos and slides to help you with your own design studios http://www.designstudiomethod.com.

Summary

- Design studios have been used by universities, consultants, and design firms for years.
- Design studios are based upon research by Alex Osborn, the father of brainstorming.
- Three characteristics of designs studios:
  - o People generate ideas by sketching their concepts.
  - o A group comes together to show and critique other people's sketches.
  - o Based upon feedback, concepts get refined.
- Advantages of design studios include:
  - o They are fast. No special skills needed.
  - o Helping you to understand complex problems.
  - o Allowing you to share knowledge.
  - o Promoting team cohesiveness.
  - o Getting early commitment on design direction.
  - o Overcoming communication barriers.
- Business barriers can be external or internal.
  - o External barriers include new laws, court cases, or new competitors.
  - o External barriers can be hard to overcome.
  - o Internal barriers are forces within your company (time, money, resources).
  - o You may be able to overcome an internal business barrier.
- Design studios maximize your design freedom at the start of a project.
- Design studios can prevent an escalation of commitment.
- Personal barriers are mental blocks by individuals. To overcome them, tell people:
  - o "Design studios are fun and interactive."
  - o "Design studios need your participation."
  - o "Design studios save you time."
  - o "Your sketches do not have to be perfect."
  - o "Design studios are research-based They work."
- Design studios require creative and critical thinking:
  - o Creative thinking involves generating ideas, using your intuition, embracing ambiguity, and using your imagination.
  - o Critical thinking involves a careful and constructive evaluation of the sketches. People use positive and negative judgment when critiquing ideas.

- The book contains three parts:
  - o Part 1 covers the processes of a design studio.
  - o Part 2 covers step-by-step procedures of a design studio.
  - o Part 3 covers advanced topics for a design studio.
- How to use this book:
  - o Each chapter has quotes, stories, pictures, tips, and examples.
  - o First-time readers should read it cover to cover.
  - o Second-time readers should use the Summary section in each chapter.

CHAPTER 2

Creative Thinking in a Design Studio

As mentioned earlier, design studios require creative and critical thinking. In this chapter, you will learn about the importance of creative thinking, rules for generating ideas, and some practical ways to generate your sketches. In Chapter 3, you will learn practical ways to produce sketches to make them easier for your participants to critique.

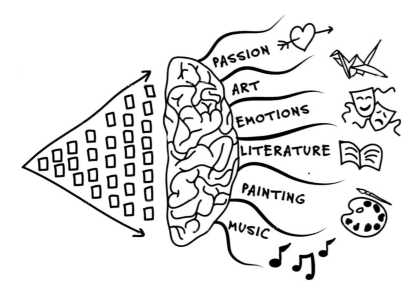

What Is Creative Thinking?

Creative thinking involves generating ideas, using your intuition, embracing ambiguity, using your imagination, and searching for meaningful connections. Creative thinking is a divergent process, where you start with a specific question and generate a variety of ideas. You perform many creative thinking activities in a design studio:

1. You determine a starting point for your sketches.

2. Participants initially sketch their ideas alone.

3. After seeing the sketches, participants critique the ideas.

4. New sketches get produced based upon lessons learned.

5. When a consensus is reached, people merge (or mash up) ideas on a whiteboard.

The goal of creative thinking in a design studio is to generate a variety of sketches, which participants will use to solve a business problem.

The Primary Purpose of Creative Thinking

The primary goal of creative thinking is to get out of the common response zone. You will never create innovative ideas in the common response zone. Have you ever been in a business meeting where someone likes the first or second idea they hear? For the next hour, you watch, in horror, as your co-workers develop an unimaginative, boring idea. In your mind, you know your customers will not like this idea. The common response zone is just a series of iterations on a single concept.

The common response zone is an iteration; it is not innovation.

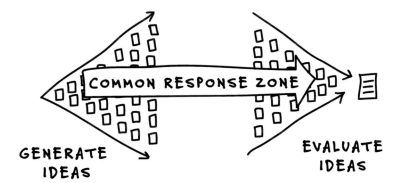

Design studios are an innovation method to force you out of the common response zone. Participants must use creative and critical thinking to produce innovative solutions. You will rarely, if ever, end up using the first or second idea shown to the group. In their work, Osborn and Parnes established specific rules to help guide teams as they perform creative and critical thinking. Based upon my experience, design studio projects are more successful when participants use the rules and tools for generating and evaluating ideas (or sketches) developed by Osborn and Parnes.[1] For the rest of this chapter, we will review these rules and tools and how to use them in a design studio.

Rules for Generating Ideas

The original work of Osborn and Parnes has been modified several times. In my design studios, I prefer to use the creative and critical rules established by Donald Treffinger, Scott Isaksen, and Brian Stead-Doval in their Creative Problem Solving (CPS) process.[2] By adapting these rules to your design studios, your participants will be more creative by producing a larger set of unique alternatives. The four rules for generating ideas include:

1. Defer Judgment.
2. Strive for Quantity.
3. Use Your Imagination.
4. Build on Other Ideas.

You can apply these four rules to your design studio projects and see tremendous results.

RULES FOR GENERATING

1. Defer Judgment

2. Strive for Quantity

3. Use Your Imagination

4. Build on Other Ideas

Rule #1: Defer Judgment

Your participants must defer positive and negative judgment when they are creating their sketches, for several reasons:

- People may sketch several variations of the same idea they view positively.
- Someone may not sketch an idea because they think the group will view it negatively.
- The evaluation of the sketches should come in a group setting.
- A participant may put more significance on an idea they view positively.
- The design studio runs the risk of staying in the common response zone.
- An unsketched idea may just need further development in the design studio.

Both positive and negative judgment can shut down a person's creativity, which can significantly impact your design studio.

The single biggest issue with positive judgment is escalation of commitment. An escalation of commitment occurs when a participant iterates on a single

"The greatest deception men suffer is from their own opinions."
– Leonardo da Vinci

idea they view in a positive manner. As you spend more time developing an idea, you increase your level of commitment to it. In a design studio, a participant decides to tweak a single concept. After spending several hours developing multiple sketches of one idea, participants feel committed to it because they have spent a lot of effort thinking and producing their sketches. Instead of sketching five or six different sketches, participants spent their time on developing a single concept. Their positive judgment shut them down!

The biggest issue with negative judgment is the sin of omission. The "sin of omission" occurs when a participant does not sketch an idea because they feel their idea will be instantly rejected. They dismiss the idea before it gets developed or evaluated. Ironically, the best ideas take time to develop. Based upon my experience, the final decisions from a design studio occur by combining a variety of ideas shown by different people. As it turns out, the unsketched idea may just need to be refined.

HOW TO GET PARTICIPANTS TO DEFER JUDGMENT

Remind your participants to defer positive and negative judgment when they sketch. The rule to defer judgment is closely tied to this rule to strive for quantity. Positive judgment can lead to an escalation of commitment, where someone iterates the same basic idea. In this respect, this person stops generating original ideas. On the other hand, negative judgment can lead to the sin of omission, where someone does not sketch an idea because they think it will be rejected. In both cases, creativity is impacted. Tell participants to just sketch out their idea to increase the quantity of ideas.

A silly idea may actually lead to a meaningful conversation. During a design studio for a mobile app, a participant told us how she really struggled to come up with her fifth idea. So, she showed the group a sketch of a smartphone with a catapult on it. Ironically, her sketch forced the group to ask some important questions:

*   What information could we throw at the customers?
*   What types of push marketing could we do?
*   What information could we just throw away (or hide)?
*   What features were important to the customers?
*   Where could we use gamification in our mobile app?

The sketch of a mobile app with a catapult was the catalyst to these discussions. In some cases, the value of a sketch is the group discussion. When I tell this story to participants, I always say, "For silly ideas, the currency is in the conversations."

DESIGN LIKE DA VINCI: DEFER JUDGMENT WHEN YOU SKETCH

Leonardo da Vinci's The Last Supper *captures the reaction of the disciples of Jesus, when he tells them that someone at the dinner party will betray him. In his notebooks, da Vinci sketched the disciples in various positions to try to capture their mindset in his masterpiece. Da Vinci struggled for years with painting the face of Jesus, which he called perfection, and Judas, which he called pure evil. Da Vinci's negative judgment stifled his ability to finish* The Last Supper. *It took him three years to finish it!*

Luckily, your participants are only producing sketches in a Design Studio.

Da Vinci's The Last Supper.

Rule #2: Strive for Quantity

You must generate a large set of ideas to produce a high-quality solution. In other words, quantity leads to quality. Let's assume we are designing a new feature for a banking site or app. A typical thought process might be to

1. **Copy Competitors.** You see how other banks and financial institutions have solved this problem. The first sketch mimics their design. So, you slightly tweak your existing design.

2. **Review a Similar Industry.** You might research how another industry is solving a similar problem. How are e-commerce sites solving your banking issue? Your next sketch mimics their solution.

3. **Mimic a Popular Brand.** You might review the designs of popular sites or apps. In one design studio, a person sketched features of a popular social site. While interesting, his sketch was rejected. However, the group did have some meaningful discussions.

While these solutions might be viable, they exist in the common response zone. You increase your chance of creating an innovative solution by generating a large number of different options. You will not create an interesting, intriguing, or innovative idea in the common response zone.

Simply put, quantity leads to quality.

HOW TO INCREASE QUANTITY IN DESIGN STUDIOS

In your design studios, you need to make sure the sketches represent unique options rather than slight tweaks to one concept. Based on my experience, you can structure your design studios to easily generate a large set of unique ideas. If you can, assemble a multi-disciplinary team of five or six people. You will want people from different roles—Developer, Marketer, Designer, Quality Assurance, Business Analyst, and so on. The different roles ensure your team looks at a problem with their unique perspectives. The Sketchers will produce five to seven unique concepts alone. The team meets to review the sketched concepts, which might be as many as 50 different ideas.

When your team has one Designer or you own a small business with just a few people, you can adapt the design studio to generate a larger quantity of ideas. If you have only one Designer, you should have them lead the design studio and the other people sketch. In this respect, the Designer gets the feedback they need to produce a better wireframe. Plus, you eliminate the excuse of sketching being the sole responsibility of the Designer. For a small business, you can ask for input from your suppliers, partners, and customers. In the end, the goal is to strive for quantity to find the best option.

PRODUCE LIKE PICASSO: QUANTITY LEADS TO QUALITY

Pablo Picasso is considered to be one of the greatest artists of the 20th Century by many art scholars. During his 75-year career, Picasso produced over 147,800 pieces of art. To put this number into perspective, consider these interesting facts about Picasso's productivity:

- *On average, Picasso completed seven projects every day during his career.*
- *10 of the top 50 paintings sold at auction were produced by Picasso.*
- *His anti-war masterpiece called* Guernica *is considered priceless.*
- *The Louvre in Paris holds 35,000 pieces of art—less than 25% of Picasso's output.*

During his career, Picasso was known to sketch in journals before painting portraits, sculpting large outdoor pieces, etching lithographs, or creating ceramics. For Guernica, he produced over 40 sketches before he started painting anything. To produce like Picasso, make sketching part of your design process and understand that quantity leads to quality.

"To invent, you need a good imagination and a pile of junk."
– Thomas Edison

Rule #3: Use Your Imagination

To get out of the common response zone, you need to engage your imagination. With this rule, you give yourself the permission to be wild, crazy, and playful. You are not concerned with the technical feasibility of an idea, when you engage your imagination. One person's crazy idea becomes the catalyst for another person's inspiration or innovation. As mentioned earlier, the common response zone is the place where most people iterate on common solutions. You need to challenge your participants to stretch beyond their normal comfort zone. They must engage their imaginations.

Based upon my experience, you can get participants to engage their imaginations by having them sketch five or six different ideas. The number of sketches forces people to use their imaginations because they must move beyond just tweaking the existing design or copying their competitor. By making people create unique sketches, you force them to think beyond their normal parameters and use their imaginations.

IMAGINE LIKE EDISON: SEEING THE LIGHT

When Thomas Edison was born, the only sources of light in homes were candles, fireplaces, torches, gas lamps, and light bulbs (which lasted a few minutes). The electric grid did not exist. People had to make their own electricity. Edison imagined a world where an electrical grid could power homes, which would be filled with electric light bulbs. It took him over 1,000 attempts before he successfully created the incandescent light bulb. Then, he needed to engineer an electrical grid to power all of the homes of his new customers.

PROVEN WAYS TO GENERATE IDEAS

In my design studios, I like to tell participants of five ways they can generate ideas.

1. Competitive Analysis

2. SCAMPER

3. Force Fitting

4. Nature Walk

5. Similar Industry

In your design studios, some business professionals will find the task of generating ideas scary. While not an exhaustive list, the following design strategies provide them with some proven methods to generate ideas.

1. **Competitive Analysis.** Review the site, app, or product of a direct competitor to see what data, features, or workflows you can adapt on your project. Many participants will already know some of this information. You can easily spot elements from competitors in many of the early sketches.

2. **SCAMPER.** Alex Osborn (1953) developed a series of "idea-spurring questions" to help you expand your search for new ideas. Four decades later, Bob Eberle (1996)[3] would create SCAMPER, an easy-to-remember acronym for:

   - S **S**ubstitute
   - C **C**ombine
   - A **A**dapt
   - M **M**agnify or **M**inimize

- P   **P**ut to Another Use
- E   **E**liminate
- R   **R**everse or **R**earrange

Use SCAMPER to think about your problem in a different way, especially when you (or your team) seem to be stuck in the same mode of thinking.

3. **Force Fitting.** In this approach, you take different, unrelated objects and try to combine them into a new concept. You can find unrelated objects by walking around a mall, reading product reviews, scanning magazine ads, or looking at everyday things. Once you find an unrelated object, try to force fit it into your idea.

4. **Nature Walk.** Leonardo da Vinci would look at natural objects for design inspiration. In addition, sustainable design takes into consideration the impact a product has on the Earth. Take a walk outside or look at another natural location. A change of scenery can lead to a fresh, new idea.

5. **Similar Industry.** You may be able to use an existing solution from a different industry. For example, Steve Jobs adapted the Ritz-Carlton customer service experience to the Apple Store. In both places, a person greets you at the door, with a nearby bar. The Ritz-Carlton dispenses beer; the Apple Store dispenses advice.

While many other idea-generating tools exist, these five tools yield the most creative ideas in design studios.

Rule #4: Build on Other Ideas

"At IDEO, the most important rule is to build upon the ideas of others."
– Tim Brown

Creative people find ways to combine and extend upon the ideas of other people. The purpose of this rule is to encourage you (or your group) to make new connections between different ideas to find innovative solutions. In some cases, you will take small elements from other sites or apps to tweak an existing idea. At other times, you might have three different concepts you want to combine into a single concept. By challenging participants to find new combinations, you will ensure a greater quantity of ideas. Plus, you should see a variety of ideas in your design studios.

HOW TO GET PEOPLE TO SEEK NEW COMBINATIONS

While creative people enjoy finding new combinations, other people find it difficult to combine and extend upon the ideas of others. To encourage participants to create new combinations, you can do one or more of the following things:

1   Explain how new combinations are part of the creative process.

2   Use Competitive Analysis, SCAMPER, Force Fitting, Nature Walk, or Similar Industry to create new combinations.

3   Add or eliminate something about the current design.

4 Rearrange the elements on a page to a new location.

5 Minimize or maximize an element on the current design.

6 Give an example of a new combination, such as fusion cuisine (example: Tex-Mex).

For non-creative professionals, thinking about new combinations may not be a natural task. Once they get started, you will notice how they enjoy finding new combinations.

WAYS TO GET NEW COMBINATIONS IN A DESIGN STUDIO

Your participants have three opportunities to find new combinations and connections:

1. **Before the Design Studio.** Before they create their sketches, encourage participants to do some research. They can interview experts, review competitors, do a field study, and more. Encourage participants to look beyond their own industry, too.

2. **During the Design Studio.** After everyone shows their sketches, the participants will see some concepts they will want to use in their future sketches. They should be encouraged to take the best design elements and combine them into a new sketch.

3. **Creating the Final Design(s).** As they reach consensus, the group ends up merging several ideas into a final mockup, which gets sketched on a whiteboard. At this important stage, they should actively combine the best elements into a single concept.

After a Designer renders the final sketch into a mockup, your participants should no longer seek new combinations. Instead, they should review it for technical accuracy and completeness. Additional design elements may be refined, but participants should no longer be trying to significantly enhance the mockup by combining additional elements.

DESIGN LIKE DA VINCI: LEONARDO'S PET DRAGON

According to one biographer, Leonardo da Vinci had a pet dragon. Leonardo's father asked his teenage son to paint a dragon shield for one of his customers. After a few days, Leonardo's father went to his son's room to check his progress. A horrible smell was emanating from Leonardo's room.

His father opened the door. The stench made his eyes water. In his son's room, he saw sketches littered about. In one corner, Leonardo was looking into a wooden box. In the other corner his father saw a beautiful dragon shield.

It was the perfect painting of the mythical creature. It was complete with a snout, piercing eyes, and wings. Smoke and fire encircled the dragon depicted on the shield.

Leonardo's father was shocked. He asked Leonardo about his inspiration. To his surprise, Leonardo told his father that he caught a baby dragon in their garden. And he put it in the wooden box.

Leonardo's father decided to open the wooden box. When he looked inside, he saw a tiny creature that resembled the dragon on the shield. It had a long tail, beard, scales, and wings. He saw vibrant green, red, and yellow on this small monster.

When he reached to pick it up, the dragon scurried to a corner!

According to Vasares, a personal friend and biographer of Leonardo da Vinci, the young artist had found a small lizard in his garden. To create the illusion of a mythical dragon, Leonardo had combined the body parts of other animals—fish scales, a rooster's beard, a snake's tail, and bat wings.

The various body part were attached to the lizard. Leonardo meticulously painted the lizard, so the colors blended. The young artist even created a support structure for the wings, so they flapped when his pet dragon moved.

Leonardo created his pet dragon by using new combinations.

Summary

- You must generate and evaluate ideas in a design studio.
- Four Rules for Generating Ideas:
    o   Rule #1: Defer Judgment.
    o   Rule #2: Strive for Quantity.
    o   Rule #3: Use Your Imagination.
    o   Rule #4: Build on Other Ideas.
- Ways to Generate Ideas:
    o   Tool #1: Competitive Analysis.
    o   Tool #2: The SCAMPER Method.
    o   Tool #3: Force Fitting.
    o   Tool #4: Nature Walk.
    o   Tool #5: Similar Industry.

Notes

1   Osborn, Alex F. (1953) *Applied imagination: Principles and procedures of creative problem-solving.* New York: Charles Scribner's Sons, 1953.
2   Isaksen, S.G., Dorval, K.B., & Treffinger, D.J. (2011). *Creative approaches to problem solving: A framework for innovation and change* (3rd edn.). Thousand Oaks, CA: SAGE.
3   Eberle, Bob. (1996). *Scamper: Creative games and activities for imagination development*. Prufrock Press, Inc.

CHAPTER 3

Creative Thinking with Sketches

Some people are afraid to sketch. You must help participants to overcome this fear. As mentioned earlier, lack of knowledge, fear of rejection, insecurities, procrastination, time management, and perfectionism are common excuses people make for not sketching. When you encounter personal resistance from someone, you can use a couple of strategies to get people to keep calm and sketch on.

In this chapter, we will focus on sketching and its importance in visual thinking. We will review critiquing in the next few chapters.

"In a Design Studio, the main artifact of creative thinking is your sketches."
– A.J. Wood

Ways to Motivate People to Sketch

When you encounter a person who is resistant to sketching, here are six ways you might convince them of the advantages of sketching in a design studio:

1. **Sketching is fun and interactive.** Unlike dull, boring meetings where you talk and revisit past decisions, sketching is fun, interactive, and engaging. In a design studio, people sketch, evaluate ideas, and make decisions.

2. **Sketching is visual thinking.** Stop worrying about documenting all your customer requirements. Instead, make a quick sketch. Add some annotations. Show your inner thoughts visually to your project team.

3. **Only people who sketch can critique.** Criticizing is easier than creating. In my design studios, only people who sketch critique another person's sketch. It is a reward for sketching. People do not want to be left out.

4. **Sketching saves you time.** Design studios are a great way to kickstart a project. Sketching is a problem-solving activity. Participants rally behind a common vision to share with their customers, team, and managers.

5. **Your sketches do not have to be pixel perfect.** Your sketches will be rough ideas. They do not have to be pixel perfect! The final sketch is given to a designer to render a high-quality digital asset. Sketches are iterations of ideas.

6. **No special skills are required.** No technical knowledge is required to produce a sketch. You put a marker on paper to draw your idea. Sketching is meant to be quick, disposable, and cheap.

You can probably think of many other arguments to persuade people about the value of sketching. In the next section, we will actually have them draw some simple sketches.

Fundamentals of Sketching

It is amazing how simple shapes and a few words can bring your ideas to life. When someone tells me they are afraid to sketch, I will quickly draw the following illustration to show the six fundamentals of sketching.

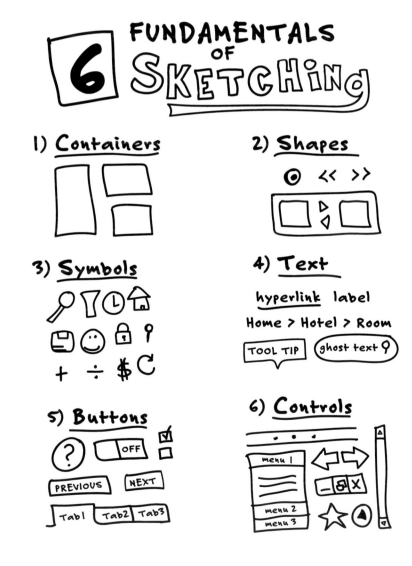

As I am drawing the "Six Fundamentals of Sketching" illustration, I explain the importance of each of the sketching elements:

- **Containers**. Use containers to show the location and grouping of your data. A large container will contain other smaller containers. I encourage people to sketch their containers first to provide an underlying structure to their design.

- **Shapes**. Different shapes make your designs more intuitive. Circles, squares, triangles, and lines can help to show relationships, groupings, user controls, similarities, and differences. These elements literally "shape" your sketch.

- **Symbols**. Iconic symbols act as visual shortcuts for your customers. Your customers click icon buttons on your site or app to access certain features, such as a computer disk to save a file or a calendar icon to select a date range.

- **Text**. Your customers scan, read, search, type, click, tap, and hover over text to better understand what interests them on your site or app. For many people, reading text is their preferred way of learning.

- **Buttons**. When your customers perform a task, they click a button on your site or tap it on their smartphone or tablet. Buttons represent actions, so they are usually labeled with verbs.

- **Controls**. When your customers want to manipulate their screen, they use controls. Users will scroll down, scroll up, separate data, sort it, filter their search, make text bold, and more. Customers feel empowered with controls.

During the explanation and sketching, I will ask people to help me. What is their favorite control? Do they have an example of a button? In some cases, I have them draw it (mainly, to get them comfortable with sketching). Then, we sketch an interface together.

How to Sketch a User Interface

Let's review an example for selecting a hotel on a mobile site, to illustrate the steps it takes to create a meaningful sketch in a design studio:

1. Develop the containers for your content, buttons, and features.

2. Add lines, symbols, and other shapes to provide additional details.

3. Write out labels for key areas and buttons.

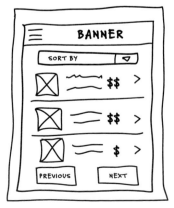

4. Add a title and description for the sketch.

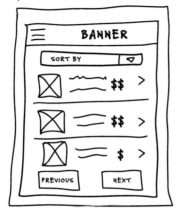

5. Use arrows and annotations for additional explanations, if needed.

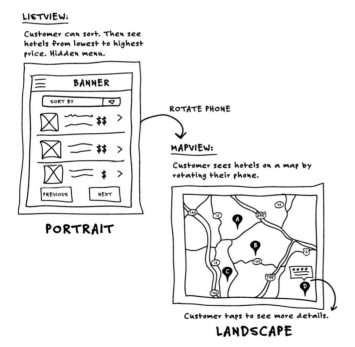

A picture is worth a thousand words. When you add words to a sketch, it is more usable. Design studio participants can scan the drawing, read your annotations, and quickly interpret it. While it may take you several hours to think up your sketch, you can produce a meaningful sketch in a few minutes.

By following the steps shown in this section, you create more usable sketches.

A picture is worth a thousand words, but a sketch with a few words equals clarity!

10 Ways to Make Your Sketches Usable

When you evaluate sketches in a design studio, you want them to be presentable. Your participants should sketch different ideas in a similar fashion. In a design studio, make the focus on navigation, information design, interactions, usability, and flow to optimize the user experience. Using the final sketch from your design studio, a designer adds visual appeal, branding, style guides, and color to optimize the business objectives of your site or app. To ensure the success of your design studios, use these 10 guidelines to make usable sketches with your design studios:

1. Sketch a wireframe.
2. Draw one concept per page.
3. Do not use special paper.
4. Use black markers on white paper.
5. Do not use a computer for sketching.
6. Do not color sketches.
7. Use a title and description.
8. Use annotations to provide clarity.
9. Use arrows to show interactions.
10. Use sticky notes sparingly.

Let's review each of these guidelines now.

RULE #1: SKETCH A WIREFRAME

You will need to explain how to draw a wireframe to the non-designers sketching in your design studios. Each profession has its own visual assets. Marketers draw storyboards, personas, and infographics. Database Administrators draw flowcharts. Developers draw entity relationship diagrams and data flows. Quality Assurance Engineers build tables and create presentations. Designers sketch wireframes.

Design Studio participants need to understand that their wireframes greatly impact the customer experience. For most consumers, the interface is your product. They do not see how data flows between various parts of the system. And, they do not care how you make your product work.

Consumers enter data on the interface and wait for something to happen— processing a request, an error message, a status update, or a confirmation. The consumer acts and reacts to your interface.

RULE #1: SKETCH A WIREFRAME

FLOWCHART   STORYBOARD   WIREFRAME

In design studios, some participants will not understand the term "wireframe." These professionals may not work with designers or developers. They may perform different activities, which gives them a unique insight into a design problem or new opportunity. You may need to educate non-designers about the importance of creating and evaluating wireframes.

The act of sketching a wireframe is a creative problem-solving process. It is a visual representation of a potential solution. Their sketches (or wireframes) should focus on user interface elements, such as navigation, layout, interactions, flow, and data. Since you want everyone to evaluate similar sketches, show an example of a basic wireframe that contains these elements: title, description, user interface sketch, annotations, and arrows.

For the non-designers, explain how each of the wireframe elements serves a specific purpose. The title names a specific concept or page within a flow. The description serves as a memory jogger, so participants either know what they sketched or what another person said about a particular sketch. The user interface sketch provides the illustration of a proposed design solution. Annotations provide relevant information about a design element or show the sequence of steps needed to complete a task. Arrows either point to key content or illustrate an interaction. These five simple elements—title, description, UI sketch, annotations, and arrows—lead to several hours of meaningful discussions.

RULE #2: DRAW ONE CONCEPT PER PAGE

Sketches with multiple concepts on a single page are hard to see. Tell your participants to sketch one idea per page. When you evaluate the sketches, your participants will move them around to cluster similar ideas together. When you have several different ideas on one page, you cannot cluster and a participant will end up getting out some scissors to separate the sketches.

A Wizard-style design is a typical pattern to use when you want to lead your customers step-by-step through a series of pages to complete a single task,

RULE #2: ONE CONCEPT PER PAGE

4 on 1 Page

NO

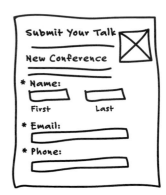

1 Concept

YES!!!

TIP #1:

Use separate sheets of paper for Wizard-style designs, too. You may change the flow!

such as uploading, cropping, inserting a caption, and storing in a photo album. Use a separate sheet of paper for each step or page in a workflow. While it represents one concept, you may find that participants want to mix and match different pages from other Wizard sketches they see. In this case, it is easier to see the sub-pages of the Wizard-style sketches on separate sheets of paper. Use tape to connect the different pages together in your Wizard-style sketches.

RULE #3: DO NOT USE SPECIAL PAPER

Paper comes in every color, size, and shape you can imagine. You write notes in a spiral notebook. You pay for goods and services with paper money. At the grocery store, cashiers pack your food in paper bags. When you open a gift, you tear through wrapping paper, open a box made from recycled paper, remove the tissue paper surrounding your gift, and look at the paper tags on your new shirt. We use special paper every day for very specific purposes.

You do not need special paper to sketch in a design studio. In fact, it is better to use basic copy paper, specifically white 8½ x 11-inch copy. Basic copy paper is readily available. You probably have some loaded in a printer near you. Everyone should use the same paper for the sake of consistency. You want to avoid the visual noise of paper with different colors, sizes, and shapes hung near each other. Plus, you want participants to be able to see the sketches, so you should opt for black markers on white paper. You want people to be able to see the sketches from across a crowded room.

RULE #3: DON'T USE SPECIAL PAPER

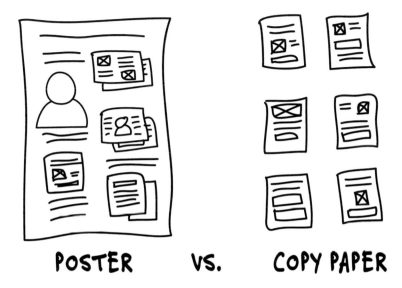

POSTER   VS.   COPY PAPER

You can use grid paper, If desired. Make sure it is the same size as the other paper used in the design studio. You want everyone to be using the same material to produce their sketches. Copy paper and grid paper are readily abundant. Plus, you can easily find them in the same size.

W.B. YEATS AND IRISH PAPER

William Butler Yeats was the first writer from Ireland to win the Nobel Prize for Literature. Unlike most Nobel-winning writers, Yeats would complete a series of masterpieces after winning the prestigious award, such as The Tower *(1928) and* The Winding Stair and Other Poems *(1929). Yeats printed many of his works on "Irish paper" using publishing houses that he set up with his sister, Elizabeth.*

For Yeats, his desire to use "Irish paper" was both artistic and political. From an artistic viewpoint, Yeats and his sister established the Dun Emer Press to focus on Irish works of high literary value. Their first publication was In the Seven Woods *by W.B. Yeats. From a political perspective, Yeats wanted to bring printing back to Ireland as an art form. Plus, he wanted to create jobs for his native country.*

You do not need special "paper" to appreciate a good sketch or even a great poem by W.B. Yeats. I understand the desire of Yeats to use "Irish paper" for his poems. It's just not necessary for sketching in a design studio. You can use 8½ x 11 white copy paper to produce amazing sketches in a design studio.

RULE #4: USE BLACK MARKERS ON WHITE PAPER

A penciled sketch is harder to see than a sketch done with a fat-nib marker. You have to squint to see pencil sketches from across the room or on a computer. You can easily see a sketch done with a fat-nib, black marker on white paper. These colors also provide your participants with the maximum amount of contrast, too.

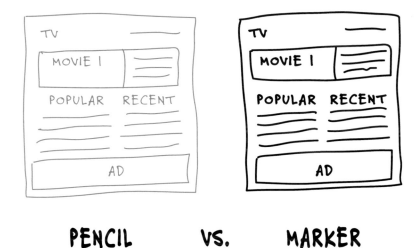

Your participants can initially use a pencil for their sketch. You just need to remind them to trace over the penciled sketch with a fat-nib, black marker to make their wireframe easier to see. In addition, you want the title, description, annotations, and arrows to be sketched with a fat-nib marker to make it easier to see when the sketches are evaluated by the group.

Different color markers can be used for annotations and voting. In my design studios, participants are equipped with a blue marker for annotations, red marker for what does not work, and a green marker for voting. Black markers provide the most contrast, so they are used for sketching.

RULE #5: DO NOT USE A COMPUTER FOR SKETCHING

Participants may want to use computer software to produce their sketches. It is easy to find software programs that mimic hand-drawn sketches, too. You should require your participants to use their imagination, hands, paper, and fat-nib markers to generate ideas. No computer program is more powerful than a person with a creative imagination.

You should encourage the use of computers before sketching. Participants should review other sites for inspiration, conduct research, and explore design pattern libraries before doing their sketches. Computers can aid participants during this research phase, but they should not be used to create the initial sketches.

Some computer programs actually mimic hand-drawn sketches. You can drag and drop common design patterns on a computer-generated palette, where you manipulate the data to look a certain way. When you use these programs, you stifle your imagination and creativity because you are tied to design patterns programmed in the software. Plus, you may not be able to find the design pattern you want to use. Finally, it is slower to create a sketch on a computer than by hand. You can easily draw two or three sketches in the time it takes to create one computer-generated sketch.

Discourage the use of sketching software in design studios. Get hands-on.

CASE STUDY: "THE COMPUTER HURT MY CREATIVITY"

In an early design studio, one of my sketchers was a Product Manager, who had been working on this particular product for 10 years. He was instructed to not use his computer, which he completely ignored. On the first day, the Product Manager displayed his "sketches" to the team. His "sketches" were screen shots of the existing pages with callouts to product requirements. In addition, his "sketches" included pasted elements from a spreadsheet program and screen shots from another website. Finally, the Product

Manager's "sketch" included a title and description, which had been typed on the page.

The Product Manager had not drawn a single item on the page. To avoid any potential display of public humiliation, I asked him to follow me into the hallway for a few minutes. I gently reminded him of a few things:

1. *You are tied down to the software program you use.*
2. *The other participants produced sketches with black markers on white paper.*
3. *He had printed out his "sketches" in full color on a high-resolution printer.*
4. *It takes longer to produce a computer-generated sketch.*
5. *His sketches looked significantly different than other people's sketches.*

The Product Manager completely agreed with me. After a few minutes, he confessed that he was afraid the other people would laugh at his drawing skills.

He agreed to sketch his ideas. After the first day, the Product Manager sketched all of his ideas. Once he had realized what he could produce by hand, he boasted, "The computer hurt my creativity!"

RULE #6: DO NOT COLOR SKETCHES

You want to discourage your participants from coloring their sketches during a Design Studio. Colors become important during the later stages of design, when branding plays a more important role. At this stage, colors distract you from your main focus. In a design studio, you want to generate sketches of a potential solution, where you can evaluate the usability, information design, workflow, navigation, placement, and data elements. As explained before, use a black, fat-nib marker to sketch on white, 8½ x 11 copy paper. During the early stages, coloring elements is a distraction. Plus, your participants are not focusing on quantity. Colors come in a later stage.

Colored sketches attract the eye more than black and white sketches. When you group sketches together, you unconsciously start to group sketches that have colors together. Since colored sketches may look more realistic, your participants may unconsciously give them more significance than black and white sketches. People may think that color indicates more thought went into the actual design. In reality, people may have simply colored their sketch because they find it fun or they were bored.

You should gently remind your participants that coloring a sketch actually wastes everyone's time and effort. As mentioned before, color distracts from the main purpose of a design studio (usability, information design, navigation, and flow). In addition, the designers are going to take the final sketch and apply a visual treatment based on an existing style guide or the design patterns they want to use. In some cases, you might be working with

RULE #6: DO NOT COLOR SKETCHES

NO   **YES!!!**

a white-label product, where one company produces a product that another company re-brands to make it match their own visual branding, style, and company policies. You need to have participants focus all their effort on the information design, not the visual design.

RULE #7: USE A TITLE AND DESCRIPTON

At some point, each sketch needs to be presented to the larger group. As a general rule, you should require a title and brief description on each sketch. A nervous presenter can simply read the title and description. If a participant is sick, someone else can present their sketches by reading their title and description.

RULE #7: USE A TITLE AND DESCRIPTION

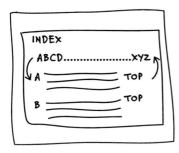 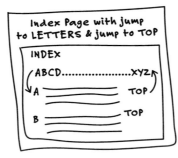

NO   **YES!!!**

Upon first glance, a sketch with a title and description may seem pretty basic. Titles and descriptions get used in many different ways in a design studio:

- Serve as a memory aid for presenters and other participants.
- Clarify the designer's intent with a specific sketch.
- A title might be used to actually name a page.
- Additional way to compare different sketches (beyond visual elements).
- Titles may become a cluster name, when you group similar sketches together.
- A description might explain an interaction you cannot see on a sketch.

In short, titles and descriptions make your sketches more user-friendly and usable.

RULE #8: USE ANNOTATIONS TO PROVIDE CLARITY

A picture is a worth a thousand words. But, pictures with words provide clarity. When you provide a picture with annotations, you have created a meaningful sketch that can be reviewed by others. Words clarify the visual thinking of any sketch. A sketch without any annotations requires people to interpret its meaning. Without annotations, your sketch might get reviewed at a later date and people may not know how to interpret it, or might misinterpret the original intent, and more.

TIP #3:

Annotations equal clarity.

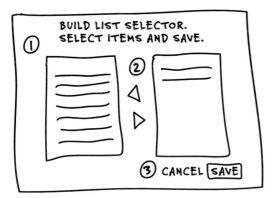

When you look at the sketch above on the left, you might be able to guess its meaning. Why should you have to guess? Use annotations to clarify your sketch.

In the right-hand image, you can see the previous sketch with annotations. The annotations point to key content. Most wireframes have the sketch in the center with annotations on the side(s). Annotations can be numbered, or you can use arrows to point to key content. The annotations give an additional layer of meaning to your sketch.

Again, a picture is worth a thousand words. Pictures with words equal clarity. Like titles and descriptions, arrows and annotations also make your sketch more usable and user-friendly. Plus, you rarely see a wireframe without arrows and annotations.

DESIGN LIKE DA VINCI: LEONARDO LOVED ANNOTATIONS

Leonardo da Vinci produced over 13,000 pages of sketches in his notebooks. Many of his sketches were wireframes, where you would see a sketch in the middle of the page with annotations on the sides to explain some important detail. Da Vinci drew over 750 sketches on human anatomy with annotations. Da Vinci was using the annotations to verify the technical accuracy and completeness of his sketches.

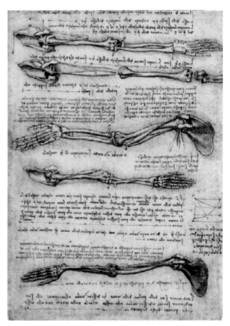

RULE #9: USE ARROWS TO SHOW INTERACTIONS

Besides annotations, you can use arrows to illustrate the steps a user might take to complete an interaction (or task). Your participants do not have to sketch multiple pages to show a simple interaction. As shown below, numbered arrows show the sequence that a user must complete to see the interaction.

Da Vinci's Studies of the Arm.

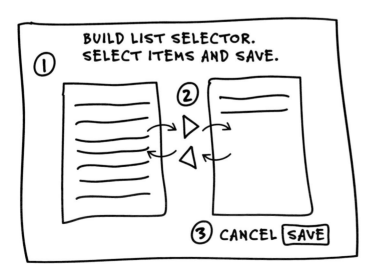

The arrows provide your team with another way to look at learnability and usability. With numbered steps, you can review the logical sequence of each step to determine the designer's intent and the intuitiveness of their sketch. Plus, you can look for any gaps. At the interaction level, you can determine if another interaction might be a better approach.

RULE #10: USE STICKY NOTES SPARINGLY

You can use sticky notes to show interactions, too. For example, you can use sticky notes to show rotating news stories or a picture gallery. Sticky notes provide a quick and easy way to show an interaction without having to redraw an entire page.

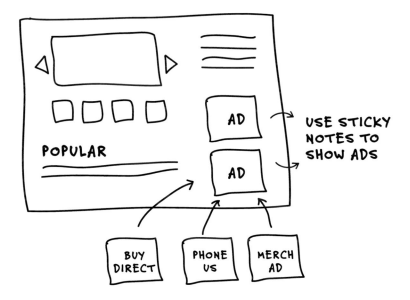

Use sticky notes sparingly. You can use arrows to show interactions. In the above example of a picture gallery, a simple explanation would be enough for most participants. Sticky notes can be used for voting or labeling a category. Finally, sticky notes do not always stick. It gets confusing when a sticky note falls off. Which sketch had this sticky note? If you do guess the right sketch, where did the sticky note actually go? Use them sparingly, because sticky notes get messy.

Summary

- Six ways to motivate people to sketch:
    1. Sketching is fun and interactive.
    2. Sketching is visual thinking.
    3. Only people who sketch can critique in a design studio.
    4. Sketching saves time.
    5. Your sketches do not have to be pixel perfect.
    6. No special skills are required.
- Six Fundamentals of Sketching:
    1. **Containers.** Containers are the content areas for your site or app.
    2. **Shapes.** Circles, squares, triangles, and lines show relationships and groupings.
    3. **Symbols.** Iconic representation of a concept (example: $ for dollar sign).
    4. **Text.** People read, scan, and study text (example: button label or blog post).
    5. **Buttons.** People use buttons to perform actions (example: print or upload).
    6. **Controls.** People use controls to manipulate their screen (example: scroll bar).
- Use these steps to show a non-designer how to sketch:
    1. Draw the containers.
    2. Add lines, symbols, and other shapes to provide additional details.
    3. Write the labels for buttons, content area, tables, and so on.
    4. Add a title and description.
    5. Use arrows and annotations for additional explanations, if needed.
- 10 Guidelines for Making Usable Sketches
    1. **Sketch a Wireframe.** Wireframes represent one person's visual thoughts. People use sketches as a communication tool for decision-making.
    2. **Draw One Concept Per Page.** You need to see each idea, so use one page per idea. Use separate pages for each sub-page of a Wizard-like solution.
    3. **Do Not Use Special Paper.** All participants should use the same type of markers and paper. White 8½ x 11 copy paper is cheap and abundant.

4. **Use Black Markers on White Paper.** Black markers on white paper provide maximum contrast for people to see the sketches. Pencil sketches are hard to see.

5. **Do Not Use a Computer for Sketching.** Sketching encourages creativity, while a computer stifles it. Use computers for research. Hand-drawn sketching is faster than using any technology, anyway.

6. **Do Not Color Sketches.** Color distracts people. Branding comes later. People will incorrectly place more significance on colored sketches.

7. **Use a Title and Description.** Titles and descriptions are used as memory aids. Plus, a title may be used as a category when the sketches are clustered.

8. **Use Annotations to Provide Clarity.** A picture is worth a thousand words. A picture with meaningful annotations provides clarity.

9. **Use Arrows to Show Interactions.** Arrows show the logical sequence of steps of an interaction. Use labels and arrows to save time.

10. **Use Sticky Notes Sparingly.** Use sticky notes to show interactions (picture gallery). They clutter up sketches and the colors distract participants. Use sticky notes for labels and voting.

CHAPTER 4

Critical Thinking in a Design Studio

After producing the sketches, participants will need to use critical thinking to evaluate them. In this chapter, you will learn about the importance of critical thinking, rules for evaluating ideas, and some practical ways to critique sketches. In Chapter 5, you will learn how to effectively move from creative thinking to critical thinking in your design studios.

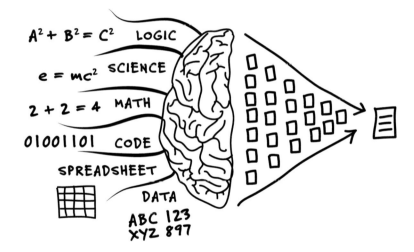

What Is Critical Thinking?

In a design studio, critical thinking involves a careful and constructive evaluation of the sketches. Participants will organize, analyze, rank, prioritize, and choose the most viable concepts to merge into a final sketch. In this respect, critical thinking is a divergent process, where you take a variety of different ideas to develop into a single, shared vision. You perform many critical thinking activities in a design studio:

1. Participants show their individual sketches to the group.

2. After seeing all the sketches, participants cluster similar ones together.

3. Each sketch gets inspected for its positive and negative attributes.

4. In the end, participants vote on the sketches to develop further.

The goal of critical thinking in a design studio is to take a variety of sketches to bring the image of the final solution sharply into view. The primary purpose of critical thinking is to get your participants to agree on a common vision by evaluating the different sketches.

Rules for Evaluating Ideas

When you evaluate ideas, your team must focus, analyze, and judge concepts to make decisions. I have adapted the evaluation rules from Isaksen, Dorval, and Treffinger's CPS process to be used in my design studios.[1] The four rules for evaluating ideas include:

1. Use Positive Judgment First.
2. Consider Novelty.
3. Narrow Deliberately.
4. Stay on Course.

By following these evaluation rules, your participants will have meaningful discussions and make effective decisions.

RULES TO EVALUATE IDEAS

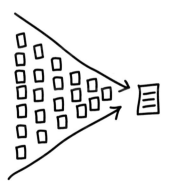

1. Positive Judgment First

2. Consider Novelty

3. Deliberately Narrow

4. Stay on Course

"The positive thinker sees the invisible, feels the intangible, and achieves the impossible."
– Winston Churchill

RULE #1: USE POSITIVE JUDGMENT FIRST

Some people love to criticize new ideas. They will tell you all the reasons why a new idea will fail. Being critical is not the same thing as critical thinking. Unlike criticism, which only finds the weaknesses of a new idea, critical thinking has you evaluate the positive and negative aspects of a concept. You use positive judgment first to explore the value and benefit of a potential idea. Then, you evaluate the negative aspects to identify any limitations or concerns with them. By critically evaluating the positive and negative aspects, you reduce the risk of prematurely discarding an idea, which could be the first iteration of your final product.

By using positive judgment first, you avoid the natural tendency of people to think negatively. Professor Roy F. Baumeister, a professor of social psychology, captured the idea of the Negativity Bias in his article "Bad Is Stronger Than Good," which appeared in *The Review of General Psychology* in 2001.[2]

> The greater power of bad events over good ones is found in everyday events, major life events (e.g. trauma), close relationship outcomes, social network patterns, interpersonal interactions, and learning processes. Bad emotions, bad parents and bad feedback have more impact than good ones. Bad impressions and bad stereotypes are quicker to form and more resistant to disconfirmation than good ones.

When people see a new idea, their natural instinct is to criticize it. By using positive judgment first, participants perform critical thinking rather than criticism. Plus, this rule helps people to be more open-minded about potential ideas.

HOW TO USE POSITIVE JUDGMENT FIRST IN A DESIGN STUDIO

When your participants first see another person's sketch, you should only have them ask questions about the designer's intent and technical clarification about an idea. As we learned earlier, participants should initially defer positive and negative judgment when other people present their sketches, because it shuts down creativity. Plus, it takes so much longer to stop and start conversations with the presentation of each sketch. After all the sketches have been shown, you will want participants to make positive and critical comments about each sketch. You should always begin with positive comments. In a later chapter, we will explain ways to streamline your positive comments.

SURE LIKE SULLY: THE MIRACLE ON THE HUDSON

Captain Chesley "Sully" Sullenberger crash-landed US Airways Flight 1549 in the Hudson River on January 15, 2009, after striking a flock of Canada geese. All the passengers were saved. The press called it "The Miracle on the Hudson." As he was landing the plane, Captain Sully used positive judgment first. They were near three boats, which would save the passengers. The flight crew followed instructions. In the end, everyone was saved.

RULE #2: CONSIDER NOVELTY

When your participants use their imagination in a design studio, you will see some wild ideas, like a catapult on a mobile app. Upon seeing some ideas, you may immediately think that they are not technically feasible or commercially viable. You need your participants to resist the urge to initially reject a potential idea. You cannot just use positive judgment, which explores the value and benefit of an idea. You must consider the novelty of an idea, too.

"First, it (a novel idea) is ridiculed. Second, it is violently opposed. Third, it is accepted as being self-evident."
– Arthur Schopenhauer

Novel ideas must depart from the status quo, which makes people feel uncomfortable. Many novel ideas will initially receive a hostile reception before being generally accepted. From our own history, consider these novel ideas that are universally accepted today:

1. **The Earth is round.** Pythagoras declared the world was round in the 6th century BC. Greek philosophers were skeptical until 330 BC, when Aristotle described the Earth as a sphere. Sailors were still afraid they would fall off the flat Earth.

2. **The heart pumps blood.** In 1628, Dr. William Harvey postulated that the heart pumps blood throughout the body and into the brain. Many of his colleagues initially rejected Harvey's theories. Bloodletting continued for several more years.

3. **"There is a market for the personal computer."** Steve Wozniak built the first personal computer, while he was working for Hewlett-Packard. When Wozniak showed his personal computer to HP business executives, they ridiculed him. Wozniak presented this invention five times. It was rejected each time.

By definition, novel ideas break with the status quo. While some novel ideas will never be technically feasible or commercially viable, other novel ideas have changed the world. It is not enough to just use positive judgment first, which is the first rule for evaluating ideas. You must consider novelty.

DREAM LIKE DISNEY: CARTOONS WITH SOUND

After seeing The Jazz Singer, *Walt Disney wanted to create an animated short with sound. Many people, including animators, were initially skeptical at this novel idea. They did not think an audience existed for cartoons. Disney arranged a test screening, where an animated short was projected on the wall of a studio. Animators, marketers, and investors were satisfied. The final product was* Steamboat Willie, *which was released to favorable reviews. The public loved their talking, whistling, and dancing mouse.*

RULE #3: NARROW DELIBERATELY

In a design studio, you need to narrow down the options presented. Quickly voting on the presented ideas should be discouraged. Your team needs time to reflect and discuss the various options presented. The leader of the design studio needs to have specific strategies and methods they can use, which the rest of the group will use to review, discuss, and narrow down the sketches. By using these explicit methods, your group can focus on analyzing the sketches and avoid any hidden agendas.

Being deliberate means being open. The Leader should explain a specific method, which the group uses to evaluate the ideas. The group should analyze the sketches using this method for a set period of time. If a method does not appear to be working, the group should discuss it, and then decide what to do next. If the method appears to be working, the Leader lets the group complete its activity or discussion.

DELIBERATE LIKE DOYLE: THE METHODS OF SHERLOCK HOLMES

In the stories of Sir Arthur Conan Doyle, Sherlock Holmes solves the mysteries by using many different methods of deduction. Holmes would analyze footprints, dirt, newspaper ads, fingerprints, dogs, or typewritten documents. Occasionally, Holmes would put his evidence on a wall to make connections and look for patterns. In every story, Holmes explains to Dr. Watson how he used a method, what he deduced from it, and the reason for his actions.

In a design studio, participants will act like Sherlock Holmes. They will use different methods, make connections, and find patterns. Like an Evidence Wall, people will put their sketches on a wall, merge ideas on a whiteboard, and more. The design studio is a methodical approach for a project team to reach a conclusion.

To quote Sherlock Holmes, "The game is afoot."

RULE #4: STAY ON COURSE

Sustained attention decreases after 10 minutes. People get distracted easily. When you spend several hours together, the group gets tired and loses focus. You want the group to stay on course, so the Leader of a design studio must focus on keeping the group focused. When the group gets distracted, the Leader must re-focus people back to more meaningful conversations and activities. Some ways to help your group maintain its focus include:

- Switching to a different activity to re-focus the group.
- Performing a recap of what has occurred.
- Exercising with the group, such as stretching or taking a brisk walk.
- Scheduling your activities to take place in 10–20-minute increments.
- Taking a break for people to use the restroom, check email, drink coffee, or smoke.

When your group loses its focus, you must take action. Your meetings will be more productive. We will discuss some ways to stay on task and maintain focus in a later chapter.

Proven Tools to Evaluate Ideas

While it might initially seem like a daunting task, evaluating ideas can be informative and fun. Before you actually vote on the different concepts, here are five ways you can evaluate the ideas generated by the group. This is not an exhaustive list, but I have used each of these methods in design studios.

FIVE TOOLS TO EVALUATE IDEAS

1. Cluster and Name

2. Hits

3. POINT Method

4. Ranking

5. Weighted Decision Table

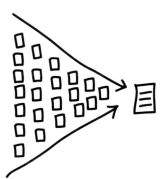

1. **Cluster and Name**. In this approach, your participants work as a team to cluster the ideas together. You may want to have them remove any duplicate ideas. After clustering the sketches, participants name the grouped sketches. You can receive some valuable insights from the clusters:
   o Which cluster has the most sketches?
   o Which cluster has the least sketches?
   o Which concept(s) has the most duplicates?
   o Do the cluster names represent any other opportunities?

2. **Hits.** In this approach, you have the participants vote on the most interesting or compelling ideas. Use sticky dots or a marker to make selections (or "hits"). You can do public or private voting, which we will review in later chapters.

3. **POINT.** The POINT approach is a four-step approach to evaluating an option. POINT is an acronym for a different way to think about an idea:
   o P   **P**luses (advantages of an idea)
   o O   **O**pportunities or **O**riginality (potentials or novelty)
   o I   **I**ssues (concerns with an idea)
   o NT   **N**ew **T**hinking (ways to overcome any issues)

   For me, the POINT method works better after you have refined the initial set of concepts. The participants have usually re-sketched their initial ideas. Plus, the POINT method follows many of the evaluation rules (use positive judgment first and consider novelty).

4. **Ranking.** When you have five to seven options, you can have your participants rank them. It is best to know the reasons for their decision. In this approach, assign a letter or number to the different options. Pass out sheets of paper to the participants. Each person ranks the options based upon their preference and provides an explanation for their decision. The Leader reads each answer and tallies the score.

5. **Weighted Decision Table.** When you have a small set of options (five to seven ideas), you can evaluate them against several factors (time, money, resources) you consider important. Your factors depend upon your project. Use these steps to build your Weighted Decision Table:

   o **Step 1:** As a team, decide on the important factors you want to consider. List them in the first column of the table.

   o **Step 2:** As a team, give a specific weight to each factor. Higher numbers mean the factor is more important. List the numbers in the second column.

   o **Step 3:** List your options across the top of the table, as separate columns. When all options are listed, your table has been built.

   o **Step 4:** Score each option against every factor to produce your own Weighted Decision Table. You can do this individually or as a team.

You can find many other ways to evaluate the sketches. On my projects, I constantly use these five evaluation methods.

How to Use these Rules in Your Design Studio

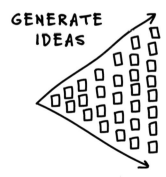

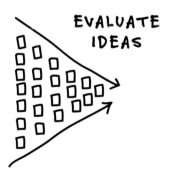

GENERATE IDEAS	EVALUATE IDEAS
1. Strive for Quantity	1. Use Positive Judgment
2. Defer Judgment	2. Consider Novelty
3. Seek New Combinations	3. Narrow Deliberately
4. Use Your Imagination	4. Stay on Course

The rules of Osborn and Parnes fit perfectly into design studios, where participants create and evaluate sketches. On my projects, I use these rules and tools for a variety of reasons:

- **Credibility.** Osborn and Parnes were two of the best thinkers in the field of creativity and innovation. Design studios are more successful using their rules and tools.

- **Structure.** The rules for generating and evaluating sketches provide a structure that makes it very easy for participants to follow and for leaders to show the way.

- **Creative Thinking Aids.** Some participants will find it hard to be creative. The five tools (Competitive Analysis, SCAMPER, Force Fitting, Nature Walk, Similar Industry) for generating ideas will help them to be more creative thinkers.

- **Critical Thinking Aids.** Everyone has a negativity bias, which affects their critical thinking. The five tools for evaluating ideas (Cluster & Name, Hits, POINT, Ranking, and Weighted Decision Table) help them to be better criticial thinkers.

- **Process Enforcement.** At the start of a design studio, I write out the rules for generating and evaluating ideas. People love rules, especially when someone else breaks them.

Design studios are more complicated than just sketching and critiquing ideas. The rules and tools described in this chapter will make your projects more successful and less stressful.

Summary

- Critical thinking gets your participants to a common vision.
- Four Rules for Evaluating Ideas:
    - o   Rule #1: Use Positive Judgment First.
    - o   Rule #2: Consider Novelty.
    - o   Rule #3: Narrow Deliberately.
    - o   Rule #4: Stay on Course.
- Tools for Evaluating Ideas:
    - o   Tool #1: Cluster and Name.
    - o   Tool #2: Hits.
    - o   Tool #3: The POINT Method.
    - o   Tool #4: Ranking.
    - o   Tool #5: Weighted Design Table.

Notes

1   Isaksen, S.G., Dorval, K.B., & Treffinger, D.J. (2011). *Creative approaches to problem solving: A framework for innovation and change* (3rd edn.). Thousand Oaks, CA: SAGE.
2   Baumeister, R.F., Bratslavsky, E., Finkenauer, C., & Vohs, K.D. (2001). Bad is stronger than good. *Review of General Psychology*, 5, 323–370.

CHAPTER 5

Controlling Conversations in a Design Studio

The hardest part of any meeting is controlling it. People talk at the same time. Opinions vary. Nobody takes notes. Emotions run strong. Some people send text messages during a meeting. Dominant personalities emerge. Someone daydreams. Hidden agendas affect the outcome. Decisions get lost in the circular conversations of people with competing interests. Now, imagine the intense meetings of a design studio, where people create and evaluate sketches.

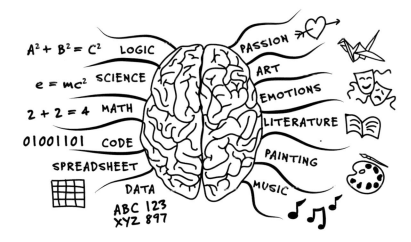

As we learned in previous chapters, the rules and tools for creative and critical thinking provide you with an overall structure for your participants. In this chapter, you will learn how to control your design studio by using the Six Thinking Hats of Edward de Bono.[1]

The power of the Six Thinking Hats is to get people to think about a problem (or solution) in the same way at the same time. Each hat represents a different type of thinking, which helps to engage the creative and evaluative sides of an individual's mind. By focusing on a specific type of thinking, your team will cover the critical details of an idea in a fast, efficient manner. Your conversations become focused and productive. Within a few hours, participants naturally use the Six Thinking Hats.

A brief definition of each of the Six Thinking Hats follows:

- Blue hat (organizing)
- White hat (neutral or facts)
- Green hat (creative)
- Yellow hat (positive)
- Black hat (critical or areas of concern)
- Red hat (choosing or emotional response)

We will review each hat in greater detail throughout the remainder of the chapter. In addition, you can use the hats in a specific order to help your participants use the lateral thinking rules and tools from the previous chapter.

Ordering of the Six Thinking Hats

As described above, each hat represents a specific way of thinking, which gets people thinking in a similar fashion with their own unique perspective. For example, you may want your project team to focus on organizing information for a few minutes. Your team consists of a Developer, Marketer, Designer, and Trainer. By telling everyone to wear the blue hat to organize the information on a web page, each person will be thinking about organizing information. And each person will bring their own unique perspective based upon their own thoughts, feelings, expertise, job role, and more.

Besides the ability to focus a group's ability to think the same way for a specific amount of time, you can order the Six Thinking Hats in a design studio to help your participants create and evaluate ideas. As shown below, you can use the blue hat (organizing), white hat (facts), and green hat (creative) with your participants when they generate ideas.

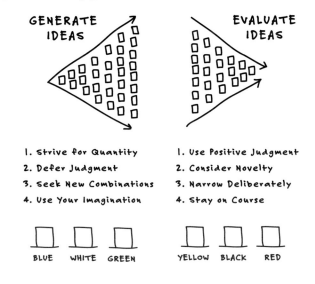

GENERATE IDEAS

1. Strive for Quantity
2. Defer Judgment
3. Seek New Combinations
4. Use Your Imagination

BLUE   WHITE   GREEN

EVALUATE IDEAS

1. Use Positive Judgment
2. Consider Novelty
3. Narrow Deliberately
4. Stay on Course

YELLOW   BLACK   RED

In addition, you can use the rules and tools for generating ideas from the previous chapter with the blue, white, and green hats to multiply your team's creative output.

In the same way, you can use the yellow hat (positive), black hat (critical), and red hat (choosing) with your participants when they evaluate their ideas. As shown below, you will want the evaluative hats to follow a specific order.

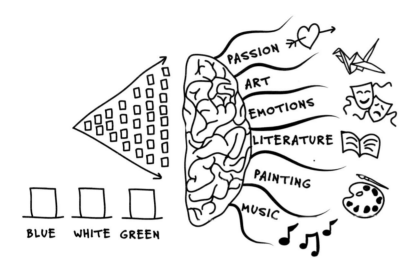

When your participants first start to evaluate the sketches, they should use yellow-hat thinking to ensure they use positive judgment first, consider the novelty of an idea, and explore the benefits of an idea. Next, your participants should use black-hat thinking to focus on finding faults with a potential idea. Lastly, your participants should use red-hat thinking to vote on the best ideas to either re-sketch or create a final mockup.

You may inadvertently dismiss a novel idea with little, or no, consideration if you use the hats out of order. In the next few sections, we will review each of the hats and how to apply them in your design studios.

Blue Hat: Organizing Information (and People)

According to Edward de Bono, blue-hat thinking focuses on managing the thinking process, keeping people on track, determining next steps, and creating action plans. The blue hat maintains discipline and focus. When you use the Six Thinking Hats, you should begin and end each sequence with blue-hat thinking. For example, the blue hat can be used to initially define a conversation. At the end of the conversation, the blue hat recaps the decision and sets up action plans.

When You Might Use the Blue Hat

In your design studios, the Leader performs blue-hat thinking to guide and focus the participants and their conversations. The Leader should be process oriented, while the participants are detail oriented. The Leader must do meta-thinking, which means they think about the next type of thinking the group needs to do. Occasionally, the Leader will need to assert control to re-focus the group during a heated exchange, so they use blue-hat thinking to guide the group back to a more meaningful point. You will see blue-hat thinking in these places:

- **Organizing People.** Blue-hat thinking is critical for organizing participants. People need to stay on task. Most of the time, the Leader wears the blue hat. The Leader focuses on how the group is interacting and what to do next.

- **Organizing Information.** Participants use the blue hat to organize information, especially during a mashup on a whiteboard for the final wireframe. Plus, participants will cluster sketches into groups after first showing them.

- **Defining the Focus.** The Leader works with participants to define the initial design problem in a white-hat meeting (to be described in the next section).

- **Determining Next Steps and/or Activities.** The Leader determines the type of thinking and/or activities to be done next in the meeting.

- **Maintaining Order.** The Leader uses the blue hat to establish order when discussions become heated or participants lose focus.

- **Clustering Sketches.** After all the sketches are presented, participants can group the sketches into clusters and name the category. For the most part, participants only wear the blue hat for this activity.

- **Recording Conclusions.** When a decision is reached, the Leader verified that it is documented. In some cases, it is as easy as taking a picture of a group of sketches.

White Hat: Understanding Your Design Problem

As mentioned previously, the biggest problem with software development is getting a team to agree to solve the same problem. White-hat thinking focuses your team on solving the same problem. When a diverse set of stakeholders agree to solve the same problem, design solutions become more inviting, intriguing, and innovative.

- **Defining the Problem.** The Leader schedules a Stakeholder Meeting, where key leaders talk about the facts needed to better understand a problem.

- **Distinguishing Facts from Opinions.** The opinions of subject matter experts may sound like facts. White-hat thinking helps you to know the difference.

- **Presenting Sketches.** People get emotional when they present their ideas. Use white-hat thinking to show sketches. Act like someone else sketched your idea.

- **Reviewing Progress.** As you progress, count the number of sketches, take pictures, record votes, and so on. These artifacts can be shown to managers and executives.

Using White-Hat Thinking in a Stakeholder Meeting

Before any sketching occurs, you should schedule a Stakeholder Meeting with the product leaders to better understand your design problem. In this meeting, you will be primarily using white-hat thinking to better understand the facts of your design problem. Some questions you might want to ask include:

- Who are your customers?
- What pages are affected?
- What is the current workflow?
- Are any analytics being collected?
- Have we done a customer survey? Usability testing?
- When do we see customers encountering this issue?
- Who will be sketching? What will they be sketching?

Using white-hat thinking in a Stakeholder Meeting helps to determine the design problem you want to solve. By getting people to solve the same problem, your design studios will be more effective.

EXPERT OPINIONS SOUND LIKE FACTS

In an early design studio, the project team included a very opinionated expert, who was extremely passionate about his customers and expertise. We had assembled seven experts for this particular project. After several minutes, the discussion paused. Our expert made the following statement: "XYZ Company does not want this feature!"

Nobody in the Stakeholder Meeting challenged this statement. After all, it came from an expert with over 10 years of experience. In addition, the expert had a strong relationship with his customers. He was very well respected on the product team, too. I was not sure if we had a strong opinion or a known fact. "How do you know XYZ Company does not want this feature?" I asked.

The expert told us a story about how he had gone to lunch with the Vice-President of Product Marketing. The expert wanted to better understand his customer, who had been in the position of Vice-President for only six months. At this lunch meeting, the new Vice-President told our expert that he did not like the idea of this new feature.

An expert opinion can sound like a fact. In this case, the reputation of the expert, his voice, experience, and customer knowledge made his opinion sound like a fact. We asked the expert to determine what other leaders at XYZ Company thought about the feature. He sent out a survey to over 200 people.

In the survey, 9 of 10 business leaders for XYZ Company wanted this feature.

Green Hat: Create Ideas (Sketch, Re-Sketch, and Mashups)

Green-hat thinking occurs when participants sketch, re-sketch, mash up or build wireframes. When participants create their sketches, you will want to gently remind them of the four rules of generating ideas:

1. Defer Judgment
2. Strive for Quantity
3. Use Your Imagination
4. Build on Other Ideas

The primary purpose of a design studio is to have people do creative problem-solving by wearing the green hat.

When they initially sketch, people should work alone. You want to provide time for people to think and reflect upon the solutions within a defined problem space. You want to avoid groupthink, which occurs when a group of people get together and agree on a solution because of peer pressure. Sketching alone provides an opportunity for people to do individual creative thinking. When the group starts to reach a consensus, participants will do a group sketching activity (or mashup) to make sure everyone agrees on the same solution. Consensus building is not the same thing as groupthink.

When You Might Use the Green Hat

In your design studios, green-hat thinking provides participants with the opportunity to generate ideas. You might use the green hat for:

- **Initial Solution Finding.** After a white-hat meeting, time is scheduled for participants to individually create initial concepts to be reviewed by the team, usually within a few days.

- **Re-sketching Initial Concepts.** Participants will re-sketch concepts based upon what they have learned from other people's sketches. These new sketches will combine elements from several sketches or be entirely new concepts.

- **Refining an Element.** You may need to focus on a single element in a design to refine it. In this case, the design studio team probably agrees on the overall layout, but there is some element that needs to be polished.

- **Fixing a Problem.** In some cases, you may want to have participants focus on creating a solution to an issue that is identified when a concept gets evaluated. In this case, participants spend a few minutes sketching solutions to the problem.

- **Mashing up a Final Concept.** When participants start to converge on a concept, you can have them sketch the final wireframe on a whiteboard together. When everyone agrees, take a picture. Send it to the designer to render a final vision.

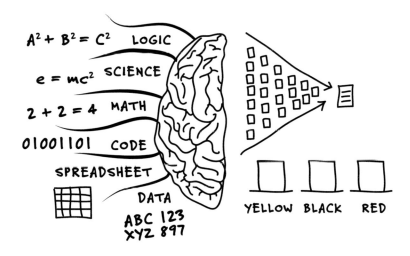

Yellow Hat: Evaluate for Value and Benefit

When the group gets together to evaluate the different concepts, they will initially present the ideas and participants can ask white-hat questions for clarity and intent. When the actual evaluation begins, participants will use yellow-hat thinking to explore the value and benefit of a potential idea. The yellow hat reviews concepts with optimism. You may want to gently remind participants of the four rules of evaluating ideas:

1. Use Positive Judgment First.
2. Consider Novelty.
3. Narrow Deliberately.
4. Stay on Course.

Yellow-hat thinking is using positive judgment first, which is the first rule for evaluating new ideas. It is a deliberate method to avoid the natural tendency of people to think negatively when they first see a concept.

In some cases, your participants may find an unattractive sketch has an underlying value that needs further refining. For example, in a workshop, the students were assigned to re-design a home page for a fitness club. One participant continually used the word "join" in her sketches. She used "join" in marketing text, headers, and button labels. This student told the group that people join a fitness club, join a class, and so on. Her main point was that people join fitness clubs, and do not get memberships. The underlying value of "joining a gym" rather than "getting a membership" made it into the final design. No other design element from the student could be found in the final design.

When You Might Use the Yellow Hat

In your design studios, you might use yellow-hat thinking to:

- **Use Positive Judgment.** After participants initially show their sketches, use yellow-hat thinking to ensure concepts are not dismissed immediately.

- **Explore for Value and Benefits.** You may want participants to see the underlying value of a concept. The technical execution of the sketch may not be what is used, but the underlying value might be worth exploring.

- **Redirect from Negative Comments.** You may need to tell participants to use yellow-hat thinking, if they start making negative comments (known as black-hat thinking) about a concept.

- **Avoid Executive Pushback.** Executives feel empowered to swoop into meetings to tell you all the reasons an idea will fail. Next time, ask the Executive to wear the yellow hat before they immediately reject your ideas.

YELLOW-HAT THINGS YOU MIGHT SAY OR HEAR:

- *Give two yellow-hat comments about this sketch.*
- *Let's explore the value and benefit now.*
- *Use positive judgment first.*
- *Consider the novelty.*
- *What are some reasons why this idea will work?*
- *Let's hold those negative comments and wear the yellow hat now.*

"The executive seagull maneuver: swoop and poop."
– Jared Spool

Black Hat: Evaluate Critically and Cautiously

In a design studio, you always want to do black-hat thinking, or thinking critically, about ideas after you have done yellow-hat thinking. When you use black-hat thinking, you want to see how well an idea solves an issue. Does the proposed idea have any issues or faults that it needs to overcome? Do you see any obstacles? What are the downsides? Critical thinking requires you to do both positive and negative evaluations to come up with viable solutions to known business problems.

Besides critically inspecting a concept, black-hat thinking needs to look cautiously. A critical inspection for technical feasibility is different than cautious exploration of potential business issues. When businesses do not proceed with caution, they risk lawsuits, damages, disaster, lives, and more. Black-hat thinking protects businesses from these potential harms. To look cautiously, you might consider your partnerships, government regulations, lawsuits, tax laws, and business strategy.

When You Might Use the Black Hat

In your design studios, you might use black-hat thinking to:

- **Assess Design Concepts.** With critical thinking, you should do positive and negative thinking. Perform black-hat thinking after completing the yellow-hat thinking. Black-hat thinking is part of the process.

- **Verify Technical Feasibility.** Your business may not have the technical capability to create the suggested idea. New hardware or software might need to be installed before the idea can move forward. Will the company make the investment?

- **Determine Fit with the Company.** When a concept is presented, you need to make sure the concept fits the circumstance. For example, a legacy-based system may not be ready for the latest technology trend.

- **Find Faults with an Idea.** An idea may not be fully realized. It might just be the first iteration of an innovation. In other cases, it may just be a bad idea. Once you find faults, you may need to see how to overcome them with green-hat thinking.

- **Scan for Potential Problems.** Any solution may inadvertently create another problem. For example, you might want to show specific examples of code on a site, but you could be giving away competitive intelligence.

> **BLACK-HAT THINGS YOU MIGHT SAY OR HEAR:**
>
> - *What are some reasons why this idea will not work?*
> - *Let's look at technical feasibility now.*
> - *Does this idea introduce the company to any risk?*
> - *Is this idea a good fit for the company?*
> - *What are some potential business problems here?*

Red Hat: Vote on Best Ideas (Emotional, Intuitive)

Red-hat thinking occurs when you need to make decisions in your design studios. Decisions will be based on several factors, such as domain knowledge, participants' own experiences, conversations about the sketches, individual feelings, their hunches, intuition, and more. In the end, each decision is a leap of faith for each person. The design studio method ensures that participants create and evaluate alternatives without jumping to quick conclusions.

For the most part, you use red-hat thinking to vote on different concepts. Voting can occur publicly or privately. In my design studios, the first round of voting is done publicly for the sake of speed and consensus-building. Usually, participants are given five votes each, if the group generates 25–30 unique concepts. It can take several hours to review 25–30 concepts. In addition, participants will look at how the other people are voting. You will typically see people voting on similar ideas, which is a natural way to build consensus.

After voting, you will want the participants to evaluate the meaning of the votes. Which sketches received the most votes? Which categories had no votes? You want to measure the buy-in, or commitment, the group has towards the different concepts. Each vote represents a decision. The discussion of the group's voting helps the participants to sort through all of the concepts they see and prioritize what the group sees as the best idea(s). Decision-making is the primary purpose of red-hat thinking.

When You Might Use the Red Hat

In your design studios, red-hat thinking is primarily used for voting, but you may need to use it for other reasons. You might use red-hat thinking to:

- **Vote on Concepts.** The primary purpose of a design studio is to make decisions on the green-hat sketches produced by the participants. You can vote publicly or privately. In either case, voting is a red-hat task.

- **Uncover Feelings.** You may encounter a situation when you need to talk about someone's intuition or feelings. Use red-hat thinking to acknowledge that feelings are present. Talk about the feelings, so the group can deal with them.

- **Probe for Hunches.** Decisions are a leap of faith based upon a person's intuition, feelings, and knowledge. Red-hat thinking allows you to test a person's hunch on the viability of innovative concepts.

- **Include Emotions in Decision-Making.** Unlike facts that can be validated, feelings and intuition cannot be verified. You do need to consider people's intuition, hunches, and feelings as components in their decisions. Not every decision is fact-based.

- **Determine the Range of Feelings.** You may need to talk about the range of feelings participants experience about a concept, especially during the later stages of a design studio. Some participants may be excited about the direction, while other people detest an idea. By understanding the extreme feelings, you may get a better understanding of potential acceptance or pushback from your customers.

RED-HAT THINGS YOU MIGHT SAY OR HEAR:

- *Let's vote on the ideas we see here.*
- *Does anyone have any red-hat emotions to share?*
- *Tell me why you voted this way.*
- *How do you think customers will feel?*
- *What pushback do you anticipate?*

Summary

- Use the Six Thinking Hats of Edward de Bono to control conversations.
- Follow a specific ordering of the hats to help your decision-making.
  o Blue, white, and green hats correspond to generating ideas.
  o Yellow, black, and red hats correspond to evaluating ideas.
- Blue hat is for organizing. Uses of the blue hat include:
  o Organizing People.
  o Organizing Information.
  o Defining the Focus.
  o Determining Next Steps and/or Activities.
  o Maintaining Order.
  o Clustering Sketches.
  o Recording Conclusions.
- White-hat thinking is neutral and fact-based. Uses of the white hat include:
  o Defining the Problem.
  o Distinguishing Facts from Opinions.
  o Presenting Sketches.
  o Reviewing Progress.
- Green-hat thinking is creative. Uses of the green hat include:
  o Initial Solution Finding.
  o Re-sketching Initial Concepts.
  o Refining an Element.
  o Fixing a Problem.
  o Mashing Up a Final Concept.
- Yellow-hat thinking is positive thinking. Uses of the yellow hat include:
  o Using Positive Judgment First.
  o Exploring for Value and Benefit.
  o Re-directing from Negative Comments.
  o Avoiding Executive Pushback.
- Black-hat thinking is critical and cautious. Uses of the black hat include:
  o Assessing Design Concepts.
  o Verifying Technical Feasibility.
  o Determining Idea Fit with the Company.
  o Finding Faults with an Idea.
  o Scanning for Potential Problems.

- Red hat is emotional and intuitive thinking. Uses of the red hat include:
  - o Voting on Concepts.
  - o Uncovering Hidden Feelings.
  - o Probing for Hunches.
  - o Including Emotions in Decision-Making.
  - o Determining a Range of Feelings.

Note

1. De Bono, Edward (1999) *Six Thinking Hats*, 2nd Edition. Back Bay Books. See also http://www.debonogroup.com/six_thinking_hats.php

CHAPTER 6

Design Studio Method Overview

I believe we can prevent usability issues with design studios.

Most of the time, usability testing occurs towards the end of product development, with little, or no, time to absorb lessons and make significant product changes. Usability testing results get prioritized into quick fixes before a product launch or future work for a later release. In both cases, a product team is treating software issues rather than preventing them. Unlike usability testing, design studios are a prevention-based method where a product team focuses on creative problem-solving, improving the user experience, and reducing (or eliminating) usability issues.

On the surface, a design studio seems like a simple task. You gather people together in the same room to sketch and critique ideas. While technically accurate, this simple description does not begin to address the complexities of:

- Dealing with difficult people and hidden agendas.
- Maintaining people's attention.
- Working with remote participants.
- Managing competing interests.
- Controlling a conversation.
- Evaluating the sketches.
- Reaching a consensus.

In the rest of this book, you will receive tips and tricks on how to overcome these complexities.

> " An ounce of prevention is worth a pound of cure."
> – Benjamin Franklin

Processes of a Design Studio

Many of the complexities of a design studio can be solved by using the various processes described in the previous chapters. Participants will use creative and critical thinking to generate and evaluate sketches. Throughout the design studio, you will have your participants use the Six Thinking Hats to control conversations. Plus, you will use the Thinking Hats in a specific order to make decisions and reach a group consensus.

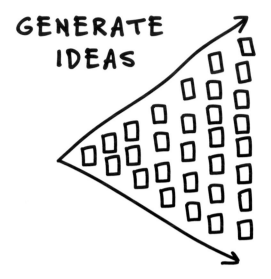

GENERATE IDEAS

1. Strive for Quantity
2. Defer Judgment
3. Seek New Combinations
4. Use Your Imagination

BLUE   WHITE   GREEN

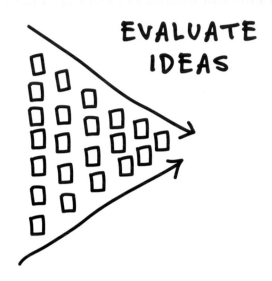

EVALUATE IDEAS

1. Use Positive Judgment
2. Consider Novelty
3. Narrow Deliberately
4. Stay on Course

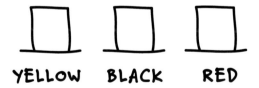

YELLOW   BLACK   RED

I always draw the above illustrations where participants work together. They refer to the different rules, Thinking Hats, and sketches throughout the design studio. The illustration helps to remind everyone of the processes. Within a few hours, people will naturally use (and enjoy) the Thinking Hats.

By the end of the design studio, some people can actually recite the rules. Containers, shapes, symbols, text, buttons, and controls become common terms used when people create and evaluate sketches, too. People love processes.

6 FUNDAMENTALS OF SKETCHING

1) Containers

2) Shapes

3) Symbols

4) Text

hyperlink   label

Home > Hotel > Room

TOOL TIP   ghost text

5) Buttons

? OFF ☑ ☐

PREVIOUS   NEXT

Tab1 Tab2 Tab3

6) Controls

menu 1

menu 2
menu 3

Nine Steps of a Design Studio

When I perform a design studio, the product team will go through nine different steps to reach a consensus. In some cases, the design studios can take a few hours, several days, or weeks to complete. It really depends upon the size and complexity of the problems you want to solve. The following illustration shows the different steps of a typical design studio.

1. Determine Need

2. Define Design Problem

3. Assign Roles

4. Perform Research

5. Generate Sketches

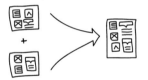

6. Evaluate Sketches

7. Vote

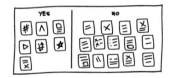

8. Mashup

9. Present Mockups

Brief Explanation of Each Step

A brief explanation of each follows:

1. **Determine the Need.** When you first meet with key stakeholders, you need to determine the best approach to solve the problem. You may want to use a different method for a variety of reasons.

2. **Define Design Problem.** In this step, your goal is to help people understand the problem to be solved. For many teams, the biggest issue is getting people to solve the same problem.

3. **Assign Roles.** In my design studios, I assign three different roles with specific tasks to perform—a Leader, Sketchers, and a Historian. The roles help to divide up the work, so your design studio runs more efficiently.

4. **Perform Research.** Sketchers need time to perform user and design research to better understand a problem, ask questions, or get inspired. You should schedule time for them to do user and design research before they sketch.

5. **Generate Sketches.** People spend more time thinking about what to sketch than actually sketching. Sketchers should draw enough ideas to get out of the common response zone. They will initially sketch alone.

6. **Evaluate Sketches.** When participants evaluate sketches, they will use the Thinking Hats in a specific order to give them a structured way to make decisions. The Thinking Hats are the key communication tools used during the evaluation of the sketches.

7. **Vote.** Participants must eventually make a choice. They can do public or private voting. Only Sketchers can vote, because they have a vested interest since they have spent time producing the sketches.

8. **Mashup.** When participants reach a consensus, they will merge several ideas into one mashup, or final design. The designer will usually lead this session, with the group participating.

9. **Presenting Sketches.** After finishing the mashup, a designer will create a high-fidelity mockup of it. You should get feedback from your customers and executives. Executives can give you time, money, and resources based on a mockup.

In Part 2, you will find a chapter for each one of the steps. I recommend you read the book in its entirety. When you perform a design studio, you can refer to the appropriate chapter for any step where you might need help.

Summary

- On the surface, design studios look easy.
- Design studios have many complexities, including:
    o Dealing with difficult people and hidden agendas.
    o Maintaining people's attention.
    o Working with remote participants.
    o Managing competing interests.
    o Controlling a conversation.
    o Evaluating the sketches.
    o Reaching consensus.
- Always draw the Processes of a Design Studio, so people can see them.
- The Processes of a Design Studio include:
    o Creative thinking.
    o Critical thinking.
    o Sketching.
    o Six Thinking Hats.
- Nine Steps of a Design Studio are:
    o Determine the Need.
    o Define Design Problem.
    o Assign Roles.
    o Perform Research.
    o Generate Sketches.
    o Evaluate Sketches.
    o Vote.
    o Mashup.
    o Present Sketches.

PART 2
Procedures

CHAPTER 7

Determining the Need

In the first part of the book, you learned how the design studio method provides you with a powerful way to generate and evaluate ideas for a product team. As detailed earlier, the design studio method uses many processes:

- Creative thinking.
- Critical thinking.
- User interface sketching.
- Six Thinking Hats.

You can use these processes in nine steps for most of your design studio projects.

"It is easier to resist at the beginning than at the end."
– Leonardo da Vinci

STEP #1: Determine Need

Before you begin a design studio project, you must first determine whether it is the right method for your product. Over the past 25 years, many tools and techniques have been created to help you better understand your customers and design smarter products. In this chapter, you will learn about the best time to do a design studio and how you can use it with other methods to prevent usability issues and create innovative products.

Reasons to Not Do a Design Studio

"The time is always right to do the right thing."
– Martin Luther King, Jr.

Let's assume you hear about a cool project that may impact a significant number of customers. You want to make a difference. Based on what you have read, a design studio is a powerful method for generating and evaluating ideas using sketching. You bring this book with you to your team meeting. You talk about how wonderful it would be to do a design studio.

But, your team instantly rejects the idea.

You are surprised and disappointed. After a few minutes, you think they might be right. Not every project needs a design studio. In fact, another method might be more suitable. Here are some possible reasons to **not** do a design studio:

- **Timing.** You may encounter a product that is too close to customer release. Design, development, testing, and marketing is essentially done. In this instance, a design studio would be a bottleneck. Instead, you should do a heuristic inspection or usability testing.

- **No Design Freedom.** Some products get locked into a specific type of software, which offers little, or no, flexibility. Sometimes, customer requirements can be so rigid that you do not have design freedom. In this case, you may want to just follow industry best practices and established design patterns.

- **Lack of Participation.** Product teams may not be able to participate because of other commitments. You need a cross-functional team of people to run a successful design studio. Managers may not want their people to participate. In this case, you use one or more of the different methods described later in this chapter.

- **Fear of the Unknown.** You can encounter people who fear change or the unknown. They resist. Any new method, technology, or process is met with instant scrutiny and constant skepticism. In this case, you must educate them and find other allies. Ask them to observe a design studio by a different product team. Make them feel safe.

- **Money.** Some product teams may see a design studio as a costly expense. They may not want to pay for a person's travel expenses or time away from their job. Again, you need to educate them on how inexpensively you can run a design studio.

- **An Obvious Solution.** In some cases, a design studio might be overkill. For example, one of the findings from a usability test is your customers do not understand how to enter the date format on a simple web form. You just need to show them an example of the date format. If a simple problem appears, use an obvious solution.

- **A Better Method.** Design studios are just one method. Assume someone tells you that two different designs have been developed. They want to determine which design is most preferred. Clearly, A/B testing or a comparative usability test are better methods than a design studio. You would only create more designs in the design studio.

People will give you many other reasons for not doing a design studio. You cannot do a design studio without willing participants and without a problem to solve.

When Is the Best Time to Do a Design Studio?

The design studio method allows you to maximize your project's design freedom before an escalation of commitment occurs. Design studios are best done at the beginning of product development or before a new release cycle for many reasons:

1. Your product team is more open to design changes at this time.

2. Time, money, and resources can still be allocated.

3. The scope of the project may not have completely formed.

4. Developers do not code right away. They need to estimate their effort.

5. Marketing, Design, and Development conduct research at the start of project.

This natural delay at the start of product development or a new release cycle provides you with the perfect opportunity to do a design studio.

TIP #1:

The start of a release cycle is a great opportunity to perform a design studio.

Selling a Design Studio in Three Easy Steps

Ironically, you may have the perfect situation (timing is right, people want to participate, a complex problem) and you still have to sell the concept of a design studio. While I do not want to sound harsh, your opinion does not matter. You have to convince the key stakeholders that they should use a design studio for their product. For me, I can sell most product teams on a design studio in three easy steps:

1. Design studios complement other methods.

2. Design studios prevent usability issues.

3. Design studios are a significant part of any Master UX Plan.

Let's review each of these steps in greater detail for the remainder of the chapter.

Step 1: Design Studios Complement Other Methods

Most product teams will know this information: Product development occurs in a series of steps. Since the Industrial Revolution, businesses must plan, research, design, develop, and release their products. For software designers, many different tools, techniques, and methods have been created in the last 25 years. Based upon my experience, all of the software design methods fit into three categories:

- **User and Design Research.** User and design research helps designers understand how their customers live, work, and play. With these insights, designers can build products their customers want to use. These methods occur at the start of a project.

- **User-Centered Design.** User-Centered Design (UCD) methods focus on how customers will use a new product, while it is being designed. With these methods, designers talk directly to customers to ensure they deliver the products people want.

- **Usability Testing.** In usability testing, designers want to determine how easy a product is to use and how easy it is to learn. Usability testing occurs towards the end of product development, usually before a product gets released. With newer software development methodologies (Lean, Scrum, Agile), usability testing occurs faster with smaller feature sets.

Over the past 25 years, I have conducted over 1,000 different projects using various methods. While design studios are the most popular method in my practice, I will sometimes recommend another method more suitable to my customer's needs.

TIP #2:

A designer or usability expert can help you determine the best methods for your product. In most cases, your product will use several different methods.

The next illustration only shows a small sampling of the available design and usability methods you can use to build your products. Design studios fit nicely into user-centered design, which is the preferred approach for designers. User-centered design methods include the end-users in the design, development, and deployment of a product.

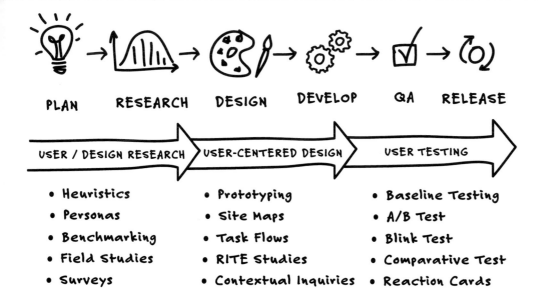

USER / DESIGN RESEARCH	USER-CENTERED DESIGN	USER TESTING
• Heuristics	• Prototyping	• Baseline Testing
• Personas	• Site Maps	• A/B Test
• Benchmarking	• Task Flows	• Blink Test
• Field Studies	• RITE Studies	• Comparative Test
• Surveys	• Contextual Inquiries	• Reaction Cards

Step 2: Design Studios Prevent Usability Issues

As I mentioned earlier, I believe we can prevent usability issues.

In my practice, I have adopted a prevention-based approach. With so many design methods and tools available, consumers should see better-designed, more usable products to make their lives easier and more enjoyable. About 70% of my projects use prevention-based methods. I firmly believe a baseline usability test before a product release should be a validation of the design and usability work that we have already done.

Prevention-based projects are activities that occur during user and design research or user-centered design. Before a product is released, the usability-testing activities can be classified as treatment-based methods, as the primary goal is to diagnose the current state of a product. Ironically, I found that comparing my design prevention philosophy to dental hygiene seems to work best for my customers. An explanation appears below.

> "Most of one's life is one prolonged effort to prevent oneself thinking."
> – Aldous Huxley

YOUR CHOICE: CHECKUP OR ROOT CANAL?

Adopting a prevention-based approach to software development can be as easy as brushing your teeth and flossing. In the last 100 years, the dental industry has adopted a prevention-based philosophy. Fluoride added to water, and waxed floss, electric toothbrushes, sugarless gum, dental strips, and other prevention-based tools are readily available to today's consumers. At the dentist's office, hygienists teach you how to use these dental products to prevent cavities. The career of dental hygienist has been created in the last 100 years.

Dentists have developed prevention-based services, too. Instead of extracting teeth, dentists try to preserve them. X-rays, caps, crowns, expanders, and braces are the most common services done on a trip to the dentist. Every effort is made to save teeth.

A usability test is like a trip to the dentist. It can be a checkup or a root canal!

We can build a Master Design and Usability Plan together. In this plan, we will lay out a series of prevention methods (like brushing and flossing your teeth), so your next trip to a usability lab resembles a checkup at the dentist's office, rather than a root canal.

What do you want? Checkup or root canal?

My customers always choose a checkup. We talk about the different methods for a few minutes and build the plan together. In these plans, I always recommend to perform a design studio to prevent usability issues and create innovative products.

Design studios are the best prevention tool available.

Step 3: Design Studios Are a Significant Part of the Master UX Plan

To complete my sell of the design studio method, I explain to my customers how design studios are a significant part of a Master UX Plan. Product Managers, Strategists, and Project Managers love hearing about plans with activities and milestones. You can download an actual version of a Master UX Plan, which I presented at the User Experience Professionals Association (UXPA) annual conference several years ago (http://www.designstudiomethod.com).

While every product is different, most projects should have these four methods in every Master UX Plan, if time permits:

- **Heuristic Evaluation**. A heuristic evaluation is a usability inspection method, where a design or usability expert indentifies potential issues with your site or app, based upon design best practices. In my practice, I use research-based design guidelines that are industry standards, which have been usability tested.

- **Design Studio.** In this approach, you gather a cross-functional team of people from various roles to generate and evaluate sketches for an upcoming software release. By focusing on design early, participants should anticipate (and prevent) usability issues before development occurs.

- **Rapid Iterative Testing Evaluation (RITE).** In a typical usability test, the design does not change. The RITE method advocates changing a design after you identify an issue. You test the updated design with the next user. If you identify another issue, you make another change and re-test.

- **Baseline Usability Test.** In this approach, you establish a baseline for what you have designed and developed. Baseline Usability Tests should occur about a month before a product is released. You can measure the performance, ease of use, error rate, and customer satisfaction. You can compare what you have developed against the current version of the product. Plus, you can fix any issues uncovered during testing.

For me, these methods provide a framework to prevent usability issues. In my humble opinion, the most important method is a design studio. The collaborative process of a design studio creates a shared vision with a focus on design and usability. With no coding needed, design studios maximize your team's design freedom.

PROJECT SPOTLIGHT: WORLD USABILITY DAY WIDGET

To better understand each of the steps of a design studio, each chapter has an explanation of the decisions made for a real-world project. In this first section, we will review the project and our first decision point, which was whether we needed to do a design studio.

Elizabeth Rosenzweig created World Usability Day to raise awareness about the importance of design and usability. Since its inception, World Usability Day has been an international event with tens of thousands of people around the globe hosting events. Events have been on every continent, except Antarctica. Annually, you can find a World Usability event in these countries: China, Brazil, Canada, Mexico, England, France, Spain, Russia, Germany, Australia, New Zealand, and the United States. Personally, I have helped to organize 15 different events on World Usability Day.

Several years ago, the theme for World Usability Day was Sustainable Design. Sustainability is a design philosophy which looks for ways to reduce the negative impacts of design on the environment for the health and well-being of humans, animals, and plants. On the World Usability Day home page, Elizabeth reserved a widget to run a promotional campaign to help educate people about the importance of sustainable design.

On our first phone call, Elizabeth and I talked about different ideas for this promotional campaign. Within 30 minutes, we had determined to do an LED light bulb giveaway to show consumers how much energy and money can be saved by switching from an incandescent to an LED bulb. Incidentally, one of my college friends worked at a company that manufactures light bulbs, lamps, lanterns, flashlights, and more. One week later, his company agreed to supply us with bulbs and handle logistics.

We had exactly four months to build the widget.

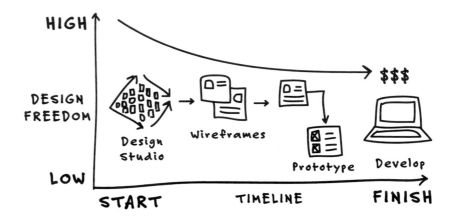

STEP 1: DETERMINING THE NEED

The first step in the design studio method is to determine whether it is the right method for your project. For the Light Bulb Widget, Elizabeth and I knew the timing was right for a design studio. With four months, we could schedule a series of design and usability projects to ensure a successful launch of the Light Bulb Widget. Our first project was a design studio.

For this project, we wanted to have several design and usability checkpoints. We were motivated because this widget would be on the World Usability home page. A brief description of the design and usability projects follows:

1. **Design Studio** (August). I created, organized, and managed a design studio workshop with 50 designers in Dallas within two weeks of our phone call. The class exercise was to create the Light Bulb Widget.

2. **RITE Study** (September). The final sketches were sent to a local designer, who created high-fidelity mockups. I tested with participants and made several changes. After one day and 20 participants, the design was finalized.

3. **Heuristic Evaluation** (October). After the mockups were updated, we asked several designers and usability experts to perform a heuristic evaluation. For the most part, these experts liked the design, but they wanted some minor changes to content.

4. **Usability Test** (late October). We updated the mockups based upon the feedback from the heuristic inspection. We performed a final usability test using some online software. We made one minor tweak after this usability test.

One week before World Usability Day, we launched the Light Bulb Widget. We received positive feedback from around the world. We raised awareness about sustainable design. Our first major project was a design studio. The first step was to determine whether to do a design studio.

I cannot imagine having done this project without a design studio.

"Design studios are the first UX project in my master plans."
– Anna Harasimiuk

Summary

- The first step is to determine whether the design studio is the right method.

- Design studios are best done towards the start of a project or new release.

- Design and Usability methods fit into three categories:
  o   User and Design Research
  o   User-Centered Design
  o   Usability Testing

- Create a Master Design and Usability Test Plan with your customers.

- Develop a prevention-based mindset with customers.

- At a minimum, 70% of your design work should be prevention-based.

- Design studios are your best prevention-based method.

CHAPTER 8

Defining Your Design Problem

The biggest problem that I see on a daily basis is people do not understand the problem they want to solve.

"Never bring the problem solving stage into the decision making stage."
– Robert H. Schuller

When confronted with a problem, most people will begin to make a series of decisions to solve it. Problem-solving and decision-making are two separate activities:

- **Problem-Solving:** Problem-solving consists of evaluating the potential causes of a problem. If you are developing an entirely new product, this type of thinking can be called opportunity-finding. In other words, you need to understand the problem (or opportunity) before you try to design a solution.

- **Decision-Making:** Decision-making consists of the different methods you use to resolve a problem or new opportunity. Most of the activities done in a design studio are examples of decision-making, such as sketching, presenting, evaluating, clustering sketches, voting, and mashing up a final sketch.

In this chapter, we will review the problem-solving activities of the design studio method. By understanding the problem, you can create better solutions for your customers.

Schedule a Problem-Definition Meeting

Once you know you want to do a design studio, you should get with the Product Manager to schedule a problem-definition meeting with the key stakeholders and experts on your project. This meeting serves many purposes, including:

- Defining the problem or opportunity you want to solve.
- Understanding any existing requirements or customer commitments.
- Explaining the design studio method to the key stakeholders.
- Identifying any additional information you may need to research.
- Securing alignment between the key stakeholders.
- Committing key people to specific roles in the design studio.
- Determining the schedule and scope of the design studio.

You should schedule this meeting two to four weeks before your participants show their sketches in the design studio. Your participants need to schedule their time to research, sketch, and travel.

Preparing for a Problem-Definition Meeting

"Preparation determines success."
– Marc Gilpin

To prepare for the problem-definition meeting, you should do the following things:

1. Ask meeting participants to bring relevant information about the project.
2. Send a list of all the topics to be covered in the meeting.
3. For existing products, ask for a demo of the current site and list of competitors.
4. If possible, interview customers to better understand their wants and needs.
5. Review any market research or usability testing for the product.
6. Create slides to describe the design studio (or use the slides on the companion website: http://www.designstudiomethod.com).
7. Provide participants with a copy of any relevant documents, such as business requirements, usability test results, customer support issues, and so on.

As with any project, preparation determines success.

Conducting a Problem-Definition Meeting

When you can get everyone focused on solving the same problem, magic happens.

The design studio method solves the problem(s) identified in the problem-definition meeting. In this respect, the main goal of a problem-definition meeting is to understand the problem you want to solve. You want to avoid making design decisions in this meeting. I intentionally call this event a problem-definition meeting to gently remind people to focus on the problem rather than the solution. I usually write the following words on a whiteboard before I start the problem-definition meeting:

- Problem-Definition Meeting = Problem-Solving.
- Design Studio = Decision-Making.

The product team needs to define the various problems or opportunities for people to work on in the design studio. You want people to agree to solve the same problem before doing any work.

In my problem-definition meetings, I follow the same agenda:

- **Introductions.** I do not assume everyone knows each other. People may be new, work remotely, or may have changed jobs. Everyone should know each person's role.
- **Design Studios Overview.** I show slides to explain how design studios use creative thinking, critical thinking, and sketching to solve problems.
- **Show a Real-World Example.** I use an example to show how design studios solved a real problem. The abstract concepts of design studios become more concrete.
- **Answer Questions about the Design Studio Method.** After explaining the method and showing an example, I answer any questions about design studios.
- **Define the Problem.** We discuss what we know about the problem or new opportunity we want to solve. This discussion focuses on context.
- **Document Consensus.** As you gain alignment, you should document consensus, uncertainty, and missing information. Hopefully, your consensus gives you a direction.
- **Create an Action Plan.** Develop an action plan and assign specific action items to people with an expected completion date. Action items might include assigning roles to people, booking travel, sending emails, or researching unknown items.

I have used this agenda for over six years now. These meetings last about an hour.

Presenting the Slides at the Meeting

For the sake of convenience, you can download the slides on the companion site http://www.designstudiomethod.com.

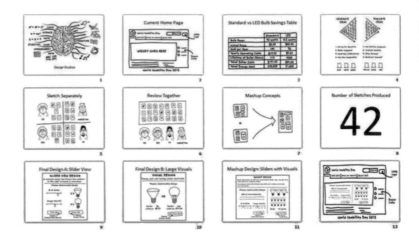

You can tweak these slides, but I do want you to attribute these slides to me. Enjoy!

Context Is King

The key to understanding any problem is context. Context involves people (your customers) and their activities at a specific point in time. As shown below, Stephen Anderson designed an interesting illustration about context.

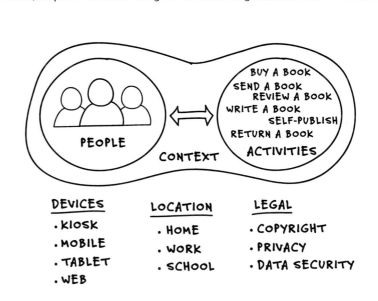

A brief explanation of each element follows.

- **People.** Independent of activities, people are individuals with their own personal behaviors, desires, motivations, habits, and more. When you consider a person's actions, you will assign them a specific role (consumer, stakeholder, job title, husband/wife, political affiliation, and so on).

- **Activities.** The things people do are their personal activities. Activities can be task-based or emotionally driven. Task-based activities have a logical objective with starting and ending points. Emotionally driven activities try to evoke an emotional response with no explicit objective.

- **Context.** Within any situation, context refers to the activities done by people. Internal and external factors impact the context of a situation. A person's mental state, their health, and belief systems are internal factors affecting context. External factors that directly affect an activity may include a person's location (outdoors/indoors) or their device (smartphone/laptop/tablet).

By understanding context, you better understand the problem you want to solve.

Questions You Can Ask

The following questions can help you to understand the context of a design problem:

1. Who are the primary people in this situation?
2. Are the secondary or tertiary people affected in this situation?
3. What are they doing in this situation? What do they want to accomplish?
4. What are their goals? Motivations? Desires?
5. Do we have an existing product? Competitor product?
6. Why do we want to develop this product?
7. What devices (smartphone, laptop, tablet) are they using?
8. Why will this product be used? How will it be used?
9. What information is missing? What do we need to research?
10. Do we have any technical constraints?
11. Where are they performing this activity? Outside/inside? Private/public?
12. How frequently do they perform this activity?
13. How do they accompolish this task now? What is their task flow? What pages are affected?
14. What do competitors do? Are there any complementary tasks? Similar experiences?
15. What are the business objectives? Funding? Commitment? Vision?

Not every question needs to be answered. These questions are some I have asked in various meetings in the past.

Questions You Need Answered

Do not leave a problem-definition meeting without these questions answered:

1. Who is going to sketch?
2. What are we going to sketch?
3. When do we want to start evaluating the sketches?
4. Do we have our list of problems and opportunities?
5. What information do we have? What information do we need?

After the Problem-Definition Meeting

As soon as possible, send out an email to the people who attended the problem-definition meeting to thank them for their participation. You will want to write out the problems or opportunities that were uncovered in the meeting, to keep people focused. Your email should include any attachments that might be helpful to people who will sketch in the design studio, such as business requirements, usability test reports, web analytics, or customer support logs. You should make all of this information available before people start to sketch.

You should work with the Product Manager to assign roles and responsibilities to the participants, such as who will generate and evaluate sketches in the design studio. In some cases, you might make these role-based decisions in the problem-definition meeting. Some managers prefer to ask their team before making a commitment. In the next chapter, we will do a more in-depth review of the roles and responsibilities in a design studio.

PROJECT SPOTLIGHT: WORLD USABILITY DAY WIDGET

As we learned in the last chapter, Elizabeth and I determined that a design studio would be an ideal approach for creating the Light Bulb Widget for the World Usability Day home page. We set up a problem-definition meeting to better understand our design problem. Within a few days, I had scheduled a conference with these key stakeholders:

- **Product Manager (Elizabeth Rosenzweig).** She was the owner of the website. Plus, she wanted to raise awareness about World Usability Day and Sustainable Design.

- **Project Manager (Brian Sullivan).** I had developed a set of design and usability activities to build and test this widget. A design studio was one of our first projects.

- **Site Administrator.** This person would help us to build the code to go on the World Usability site, which included the logistics of shipping the bulbs to consumers.

- **Light Bulb Manufacturer.** We needed some technical information about LEDs from a light bulb manufacturer, who had generously agreed to sponsor the free bulbs.

We focused this meeting on understanding the problem rather than creating a solution.

The Site Administrator provided us with several key constraints. She gave us the dimensions of the widget and the color palette used for World Usability Day. In addition, she told us of her upcoming updates to the site. With so many events being registered, she needed to focus on other areas of the site. Elizabeth and I knew this meant that the Site Administrator did not want to participate as a sketcher in the design studio. Luckily, the Site Administrator was exploring several options on how to ship the light bulbs. She planned to have this information to us within two weeks.

The light bulb manufacturer provided us with technical information on LED bulbs. They provided us with a spreadsheet to show the energy and cost savings of switching out one incandescent bulb for an LED bulb. We would use this information in our design studio.

	Standard	LED
Bulb Power	50 watts	4.2 watts
Initial Price	$2.00	$42.50
KwH per Year	146	32
Yearly Operating Costs	$15.50	$3.25
Lifetime of Bulbs (Hours)	715	5000
Total Dollar Costs	$197.50	$85.00
Total Energy Used	250,000	21,000

The light bulb manufacturer worked out with the Site Administrator how to handle shipping the bulbs to consumers.

By the end of the meeting, all of the stakeholders had set their objectives, with the steps needed to achieve them. We assigned dates to each of our action items. The Site Administrator decided to create a simple form to collect the addresses of consumers, which was necessary to ship the LED bulbs. I was going to run the design studio with a set of designers in a few weeks. Plus, I would get an updated mockup to Elizabeth using the dimensions and color palette from the Site Administrator.

I sent a follow-up email about an hour after the meeting.

Summary

- Problem-Solving and Decision-Making are two different activities.
    - o   Problem-Solving is about evaluating the potential causes of a problem.
    - o   Decision-Making is about the methods you use to resolve a problem.
- Schedule a problem-definition meeting with key stakeholders and experts.
- The problem-definition meeting should occur two to four weeks before sketches are shown.
- Participants need time to research, sketch, and travel.
- The first thing to do in the meeting is to explain the design studio method.
- Show a real-world example to make the abstract concepts more concrete.
- Focus on the context of the problem to better understand it.
- Context refers to how your customer uses your product for a specific purpose.
- Document consensus to ensure everyone solves the same problem.
- Create action plans for any unknown items or missing information.
- Action plans should have action items with assigned people and completion dates.
- Send a follow-up email documenting the meeting decisions and attach any important documents.

CHAPTER 9

Assigning Roles and Responsibilities

As soon as you determine to do a design studio, you need to decide who will participate. The product team can help you to assign roles and responsibilities to specific people.

All the world's a stage,
And all the men and women merely
    players:
They have their exits and their entrances;
And one man in his time plays many parts,
His acts being seven ages.
– William Shakespeare's *As You Like It*

Three Roles in a Design Studio

Towards the end of your problem-definition meeting, you need to ask the meeting attendees for a commitment to participate in the design studio. You should review the estimated time required and reinforce the benefits of participation. Some people will enthusiastically volunteer, while other people will be assigned.

In some cases, you may discover that a key person gets assigned to the design studio, but they were not in the problem-definition meeting. Your introductory email to this person should contain all of the necessary information to get them familiar with the problem, and to get started on their sketches. Be sure to include all your contact information, and even suggest that the new person give you a call to review the materials together.

TIP #1:

Do not assume everyone will volunteer. Some people will be assigned.

Based upon my experience, design studios should have three main roles. Each role has very specific responsibilities and divides the work between the individuals:

- **Leader.** This person guides discussions, sets expectations, schedules tasks, directs the group, tallies votes, and more. Leaders do not generate or evaluate concepts. Leaders do these types of thinking: organizing (blue hat) and explaining (white hat).

- **Sketcher.** These people generate and evaluate ideas. An individual sketches their concepts based upon guidelines described in a later chapter. Only Sketchers can critique other people's sketches. Limit the number of Sketchers to five or six people.

- **Historian**. This person assists the Leader by taking pictures, erasing whiteboards, moving furniture, getting supplies, and watching participants. Historians do not generate or evaluate concepts. In many respects, they are a counselor and witness.

Some people refer to the Historian as a Scribe, which grossly undervalues this person's effort and importance in a design studio.

Characteristics of Your Design Studio Participants

Participants in a design studio undertake a heroic mission. They actively want to solve a problem or create a new opportunity for the betterment of your customers. As shown below, each participant has their own set of unique characteristics.

Your Design Studio Heroes

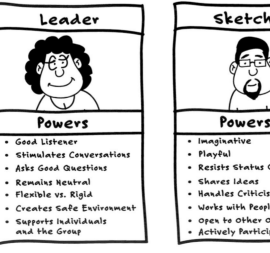

Leader

Powers
- Good Listener
- Stimulates Conversations
- Asks Good Questions
- Remains Neutral
- Flexible vs. Rigid
- Creates Safe Environment
- Supports Individuals and the Group

Sketcher

Powers
- Imaginative
- Playful
- Resists Status Quo
- Shares Ideas
- Handles Criticism
- Works with People
- Open to Other Opinions
- Actively Participates

Historian

Powers
- Wants to Collaborate
- Takes Pictures
- Looks for Patterns
- Documents Results
- Aids the Leader
- Remains Objective
- Wants to Investigate
- Passively Participates

Your design studio participants are heroes. But every hero has their flaw. When you assemble your design studio participants, use these characteristics to put people in the best possible role.

When assigning the different roles, you should consider the strengths, personalities, and job functions of your design studio participants. Based upon my experience, I have developed a set of guidelines to help me with assigning the roles in a design studio:

- Leaders should not be a supervisor or manager of another person.
- Usability, Design, and Marketing employees make good Leaders.
- You must always have one Designer as a Sketcher in a design studio.
- Product Managers and Project Managers enjoy being Historians.
- Historians should be Leaders in a future design studio.
- The Leader should have participated as Historian and Sketcher in the past.

For consistency, people must stay in their assigned role for the duration of the design studio.

TIP #2:

Consider strengths, personalities, and job functions when you assign roles.

Facilitation Is the Key to a Successful Design Studio

The Leader must have very strong facilitation skills. They must be able to actively listen, handle strong egos, adjust tactics, schedule activities, and so on. Before the design studio begins, the Leader should already have a schedule of activities for the participants. The rules for generating and evaluating give the Leader a framework for the design studio. The Leader must be engaged in the current moment, while thinking about the next steps. Leaders are listeners. They adapt based on the changing needs of each design studio and its participants.

You should plan to rotate the leadership to other people on the team for the next design studio. The Leader and Historian already have a natural mentor–apprentice relationship. If you are the Leader, plan to teach the Historian about the process and provide best practices for handling facilitation issues. If you are a Historian, you should actively watch and listen to the Leader to see how you can improve your own facilitation skills. If you are a Sketcher, you may want to consider being a Historian first before you take on the role of the Leader.

The facilitation skills of a Leader are the key to a design studio. You can plan to develop everyone to move into this role.

Assemble a Cross-Functional Team

You want to assemble a cross-functional team of experts to get different perspectives in the design studio. Your participants should come from different departments—Design, Marketing, Development, Support, Training, and so on. Employees and managers can participate. You can include customers, suppliers, and consultants from outside your company to participate, too. Different perspectives increase the likelihood of your participants creating diverse sketches.

Advantages of a Cross-Functional Team

The composition of a cross-functional team greatly increases the creative and critical thinking in your design studios. The advantages of a cross-functional team include:

- **Diversity**. With a variety of people from different departments, you will have unique perspectives based upon each person's expertise. The participants will look at the problem in a different way, so their sketches should be different.

- **Cohesion**. In a design studio, participants share a common goal to solve a problem. Participants complete assignments together using their individual talents to further the bigger goals of the team. I have seen broken teams healed in a design studio.

- **Synergy**. With a variety of perspectives, the collaboration between individuals should create a greater total effect than that of each person working alone. The interactions of the group should lead to greater creativity, as people build upon the ideas of others.

- **Consensus**. When the design studio ends, your project has a final design, or product vision. By assembling a cross-functional team, your participants are instant allies within your company for the final sketches from the design studio.

To ensure these benefits, you must choose your design studio participants wisely.

Challenges with Cross-Functional Teams

While cross-functional teams have many advantages, managing and working with different people is filled with challenges, including:

- **Competing Interests**. When you have people from different departments, you will have competing interests. Marketing wants a product released next week. QA wants to ensure the quality. The Leader must manage the competing interests of the team.

- **Hidden Agendas**. Some participants may have hidden agendas. For example, a sales person's annual bonus may be tied to a particular customer. So, their sketches are tailored for their bonus and their customer. Participants should be honest.

- **Conflict**. While diversity has its advantages, it can create conflict. Team members may not understand or care about another person's viewpoints. A negative comment can lead to hurt feelings. Passive-aggressive behavior can emerge.

- **Difficult Egos**. Some egos are so big, they fill the entire room. When a person's ego affects productivity, speak to them privately. People with big egos respect confidence, and seize upon uncertainty. Give them a centimeter, they take a kilometer.

The Leader must be able to manage the challenges of dealing with different people.

A Short Interlude

The names have been changed to protect the innocent.

A few years ago, I was working on a design studio to help a non-profit company update their customer relationship tool. We had assembled a cross-functional team, which consisted of several experts, including a person from Business Development and one from Accounts Receivables. They had different job functions and used the customer relationship tool in completely different ways. To make matters worse, their managers warned me of their competitiveness.

They fought constantly.

Both people argued passionately for their own sketches. Each person listened carefully to the other person when a sketch was presented. The Business Development person scribbled down notes and shook his head in disagreement several times. Using her smartphone, the Accounts Receivables employee only took pictures of sketches done by the Business Development person. Instead of listening to other people, she studied the pictures of his sketches.

The design studio was tense. Productivity plummeted. And, it was just 11:30 a.m.

I decided to buy them lunch. I wanted them to laugh, so I told my funny story known as "The Rabbit Story" (be sure to check the book site (http://www.designstudiomethod.com) for the whole story). They both laughed. With the tension relieved, I told the Accounts Receivables person to delete the pictures from her smartphone. It was the Historian's job to take pictures. Plus, she was not paying attention to other participants.

Then, I had a conversation with the Business Development employee. While he did not openly criticize the sketches, his body language was distracting and showed his disapproval of new ideas. I kindly asked him to stop shaking his head in disagreement. I gently reminded him to use positive judgment first when he evaluates ideas.

They both apologized to me. I asked them to apologize to each other. They did.

We had a private conversation and nice lunch. When we came back from lunch, the Business Development person was more open and reserved. The Accounts Receivables person did not pick apart the sketches in the mean-spirited way she had exhibited in the morning. In the end, the design studio was very productive.

As a Leader, you need a "Rabbit Story" to lighten the mood.

PROJECT SPOTLIGHT: WORLD USABILITY DAY WIDGET

As we learned in the last chapter, Elizabeth and I held our problem-definition meeting to better understand our design problem. By the end of the problem-definition meeting, we had determined several things about our design problem. We had:

1. Understood the dimensions of the widget on the World Usability Day site.
2. Determined how to handle shipping the free LED bulbs to consumers.
3. Developed a Master Design and Usability Test Plan.
4. Scheduled a design studio to occur two weeks after the problem-definition meeting.
5. Received a spreadsheet with the energy and cost savings of switching from an incandescent to an LED bulb.

We purposely did not brainstorm any designs for the widget because we wanted to understand the problem before we tried to solve it. Our next step was to assign roles and responsibilities.

I assumed the role of the Leader for the design studio. I had already developed training material to show participants. As the President of the Dallas chapter of UXPA, I knew over 1,000 Designers and usability professionals eager to fill the roles of the Historian and Sketchers. I sent out an email blast for participation.

My friend, Cone Johnson, immediately assumed the role of the Historian. As it turns out, Cone's demeanor is an ideal fit for this role. Cone helped me to set up the room, greet people, hand out supplies, refresh drinks, answer questions, take pictures, and tally votes. She helped to clean up at the end of the session. In some cases, the Historian may need an assistant with a large group. My son, Sean Sullivan, was Cone Johnson's helper.

We trained 50 people in this workshop, including my wife, Susan Sullivan, and son. We broke the workshop attendees into teams. Since I knew everyone, I strategically assigned people to teams to ensure diversity. One team consisted of: Taylor Cowan (Developer), Jeremy Johnson (Designer), Laura Martinez (Graphic Design), Susan Sullivan (Paralegal), Keith Anderson (Content Strategist), and Joseph Vatalaro (Student). I knew this cross-functional team would be successful at the creative and critical thinking needed for this design studio.

Our team was assembled!

Summary

- Assign these three roles in a design studio:
  - Leader
  - Sketcher
  - Historian
- Assemble a cross-functional team to get different perspectives.
- Consider strengths, personalities, and job functions when you assign roles.
- The advantages of cross-functional teams include:
  - Diversity.
  - Cohesion.
  - Synergy.
  - Consensus.
- The disadvantages of cross-functional teams include:
  - Competing interests.
  - Hidden agendas.
  - Conflict.
  - Difficult egos.
- Leaders must be able to handle intense situations.
- Use these strategies to deal with difficult people:
  - Take a break.
  - Buy them lunch.
  - Tell a joke.
  - Talk privately to individuals.
  - Remind them about the Thinking Hats and rules.
  - Always be respectful and confident.

CHAPTER 10

Performing User and Design Research

Before your participants begin sketching their ideas, you should schedule time for user and design research. Both types of research help them to understand the context of the problem they need to solve. In my design studios, I schedule several days for participants to do research.

"If we knew what it was we were doing, it would not be called research, would it?"
– Albert Einstein

STEP #4: DESIGN & USER RESEARCH

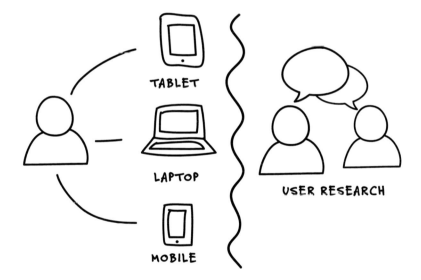

TABLET

LAPTOP

MOBILE

USER RESEARCH

A brief description of each type of research appears below:

- **User Research.** This type of research focuses more on customers than technology. Some examples of user research include reviewing surveys, interviewing customers, examining customer task flows, reading support logs, analyzing market research, or studying usability reports.

- **Design Research.** This type of research focuses on the different ways a problem has been solved using a product or service. Some examples of design research include reviewing competitor sites, examining web analytics, analyzing clickstream data, viewing design pattern libraries, and more.

Before drawing anything, you should encourage Sketchers to spend several hours, or days, doing user and design research.

What's the Difference Between User and Design Research?

The answer is, obviously, not much. Yet, it is everything.

For me, I like to specify a difference between user and design research with design studio participants to get them to think beyond the way they normally conduct research. For example, every person will use the Internet to conduct research for their career. They go to a search engine, type in their search, and press Enter. A results list appears. This type of "research" follows the same pattern: click a link, read something, click the Back button, click another link, read something else, search again, and again, and again.

While performing searches on the Internet is not inherently evil, it should not be the primary source of research for a design studio. Ideally, your team should have collected some research at the problem-definition meeting to share with the Sketchers, but I still like to challenge the Sketchers to conduct their own research as well. By using the terms "User Research" and "Design Research" with participants, I have found that it gets them to research beyond the Internet. In most cases, the Sketchers will take the time to talk with actual customers.

"Using a search engine is not the same thing as doing user and design research."
– Keith Anderson

TIP #1:

Use the terms "User Research" and "Design Research" to focus participants. Challenge them to do more than just use a search engine.

Ways to Conduct User Research

User research focuses more on customers than technology. I have seen each of these methods done before a design studio. When a participant asks about ways to conduct user research, I recommend these methods:

- **Contextual Interviews**. In this approach, you interview your customers, watch them work, take notes, and verify your observations.

- **Diary Study.** With this method, customers record their thoughts into a diary. You review their diary to better understand their thoughts while using your product.

- **Card Sorts**. Card sorting is an interactive method where your customers group information on your site or app, which ensures that your product's structure matches how users think.

- **Field Study**. This method allows you to observe customers in their natural environment, giving you a better understanding of how people work.

- **Surveys.** You can send a series of questions to your customers to help you learn how they use your site or app. I recommend using the System Usability Scale (SUS), which is a 10-question survey for the subjective evaluation of your product.

You can find many other user research methods on the Internet. Again, I like to use the term "User Research" to force people to think about talking to their customers.

Ways to Conduct Design Research

As explained earlier, design research focuses more on technology than customers. When a participant asks about ways to conduct design research, I give them these methods:

- **Heuristic Inspection**. In this method, people evaluate a site or app using a list of established design and usability guidelines.

- **Web Analytics**. With web analytics, you can see how customers use your product. You can see where customers abandon your site or app.

- **Competitive Analysis**. In this method, you compare the strengths and weaknesses of your product against your competitors. You may be inspired or see something to exploit.

- **Use Cases**. This method describes how a customer uses a particular feature of your website, which includes the steps needed to complete a task.

- **Usability Testing**. A usability test identifies user frustrations and problems with your site through one-on-one sessions with customers performing tasks on your site.

As shown above, the design research methods go beyond using an Internet search engine. In an early design studio, we actually scheduled time to review use cases, usability testing results, personas, and web analytics before participants sketched. In addition, you want this research to be available in the design studio and stored in an online location for people to review.

TIP #2:

You can schedule additional time for user and design research, if desired.

Tips for Doing Fast Design and User Research

You may not have time to conduct original user and design research. Here are some tips to quickly gather research to educate participants:

1. **Gather Existing Research.** Ask people to send the Product Manager any existing research from Usability, Design, or Market Research teams.

2. **Ask the Help Desk.** Send an email to the Help Desk to see if they can review call logs for potential customer issues.

3. **Search the Internet.** Do some quick searches to gather information—site reviews, customer comments, and any other kind of business intelligence.

4. **Review Design Pattern Libraries.** See how other designers solve different problems. Be sure to review the problem their solution solves.

5. **Ask an Expert.** If you find an article on a blog, send an email to the writer of the article with your question.

6. **Send a Survey to Customers.** Most surveys are answered within the first two days. Create your survey to get some quick information.

7. **Call Your Customers.** If possible, call a customer or ask the Account Manager to do it. Ask customers the same questions and look for patterns in their answers.

8. **Ask the Product Team.** An informal meeting with the product team can help you to gather anecdotal information (stories, presentations) that might be useful.

While original user and design research can be a great option, you can use a lot of different approaches to gather insights on your customers.

The Secret to Creativity Is Time Management

When you strip away all the myth and magic about creativity, you will see that creativity is about hard work. For most creative activities, time is spent on studying, observing, reflecting, incubating, experimenting, and verifying ideas. **The secret to creativity is time management.** Pablo Picasso created 147,800 completed works of art in his lifetime, which means he created an average of seven pieces of art every day of his 75-year career. Many people think Picasso was the greatest artist of the 20th century. Clearly, Picasso was a phenomenal time manager, too.

"Genius is 1% inspiration and 99% perspiration."
– Thomas Edison

In 1926, Graham Wallis created one of the earliest theories on creativity. According to Wallis, creativity occurs in four stages:

1. **Preparation**. A person must define the problem they want to solve, then conduct research to better understand the problem.

2. **Incubation.** After spending time researching a problem, a person should spend time letting the idea simmer in their subconscious.

3. **Illumination**. Suddenly, a new idea emerges, which may solve the problem they have studied and stewed upon for some time.

4. **Verification**. When a person creates a solution, they can verify with other people how successfully it solves the problem.

Other scholars, including Alex Osborn and Sidney Parnes, have built upon this early model of creativity from Wallis.

The following table shows how the four phases of Wallis' theory applies to a design studio.

Creativity Stage	Design Studio Activity	How It Applies
Preparation	Problem-Definition Meeting, User and Design Research	People must understand the problem to solve. People need time to study and observe.
Incubation	User and Design Research	Sketchers should reflect on the problem and their research before sketching.
Illumination	User and Design Research, Generating Sketches	Once a Sketcher gets an idea, they may want to research more or produce a sketch.
Verification	Evaluating Sketches, Voting, Re-sketching, Mashing Up	After a sketch is presented, it is evaluated and used by the design studio group.

Time spent on user and design research is critical to help your participants prepare, incubate, and illuminate their creative ideas. You must schedule this time in your planning. Your participants must understand the secret to creativity is time management, especially when you give them time for user and design research.

TIP #3:

Research helps participants to prepare, incubate, and illuminate their ideas.

Sharing Your Research

Your participants should share their research with the other design studio participants. By getting additional insights and sharing them with the team, everyone is more productive. Documents, presentations, meeting notes, pictures, and information radiators should be collected and stored by the Historian to be accessed by all participants. In an early design studio, the Historian immediately created an intranet page for participants to access. On this project, she created a one-page document referencing the hyperlinks to competitor sites, design pattern libraries, personas, and other research. Sketchers used this information right away.

TIP #4:

Store user and design research in a common location for everyone to access.

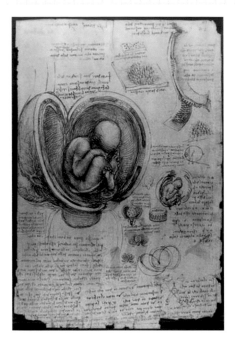

Da Vinci's Study of Embryos.

DESIGN LIKE DA VINCI: DA VINCI'S USER AND DESIGN RESEARCH: DISSECTING CADAVERS

Leonardo da Vinci has over 750 sketches on human anatomy in his notebooks.

To ensure the accuracy and completeness of his sketches, da Vinci was known to have dissected 10 cadavers to help him better understand human anatomy. Pope Leo X would eventually outlaw the dissection of cadavers, which was seen as socially repugnant. Planning to publish his sketches and observations, da Vinci would verify the sketches with an Anatomy Doctor. Unfortunately, the Anatomy Doctor (Marcontonio della Torre) died of the Black Death before publishing da Vinci's sketches.

According to Vasari, da Vinci's biographer, Leonardo, to his surprise, got permission from an old man to dissect him upon his death. When the old man started to die, Leonardo held him until his death. Within a few minutes, da Vinci started dissecting the dead man. Da Vinci wanted to know the cause of a sweet death.

Leonardo put his sketches in a codex, where they stayed for hundreds of years. Without an Internet search engine, da Vinci conducted his own user and design research.

PROJECT SPOTLIGHT: WORLD USABILITY DAY WIDGET

As we learned in the last chapter, I was conducting a design studio workshop with my friend, Cone Johnson. The workshop attendees were split into groups and roles were assigned. One group consisted of a cross-functional set of people: Paralegal, Developer, Content Strategist, Graphic Designer, Student, and Web Designer. Now we wanted our participants to conduct some user and design research. They were given two hours.

I explained the difference between user and design research to challenge people to do more than just an Internet search. We were working in a neighborhood where builders were remodeling a home. Two of our participants decided to talk with the builders, who were cordial although very busy. After 20 minutes, the participants got into their car to go to a local hardware store to talk with a helpful person in the lighting department. They came back with literature, which included three charts on how switching from an incandescent to an LED bulb saves consumers energy, time, and money.

While these attendees were away, their team reviewed various sites and apps to learn more about LED bulbs. They reviewed government, e-commerce, and lighting manufacturer sites to learn about LED lights. The Web Designer looked at some design pattern libraries to find popular ways to compare items. The Graphic Designer reviewed sites to see how energy savings could be displayed. They found slides from an electric company with some interesting visuals. Plus, the student found an interesting article on how a hotel chain was replacing all of its incandescent bulbs with LEDs, which had already resulted in large energy savings.

When the participants came back from the hardware store, the group shared their findings with each other. They were ready to begin sketching.

Summary

- Schedule time for Sketchers to conduct user and design research.
- Use the terms "user research" and "design research" to motivate participants.
- Challenge them to do more than a quick search on a search engine.
- You do not have to do original user and design research.
- Collect existing research from sales, usability, customer support, and market research.
- The secret to creativity is time management.
- User and design research helps people to prepare, incubate and illuminate their creative ideas.
- Share your research with other participants.
- The Historian should archive all research in a common location.
- Da Vinci did user and design research before sketching on human anatomy.

CHAPTER 11

Generating Sketches Separately

After conducting their user and design research, participants should initially sketch alone. You want to ensure each person gets the opportunity to be individually creative. Plus, you want to produce enough sketches to get out of the common response zone, to create something that is innovative, inviting, and intriguing.

> "Artists work best alone. I do not believe anything really revolutionary has been invented by a committee."
> – Steve Wozniak

STEP #5: GENERATE SKETCHES SEPARATELY

While your Sketchers perform user and design research, you should remind them of the **Four Rules for Generating Ideas** and the **10 Rules of Sketching**.

Four Rules for Generating Ideas

As described earlier, Osborn and Parnes created rules for generating ideas:

1. Defer Judgment
2. Strive for Quantity

3. Use Your Imagination

4. Build on Other Ideas

In my design studios, I will send an email to my participants with these four rules for generating ideas before they do their user and design research. In the same email, I provide them with the list of tools for generating ideas from Chapter 2: Competitive Analysis, SCAMPER, Force Fitting, Nature Walk, Similar Industries. When they arrive on the first day, they will see the **Four Rules for Generating Ideas** written on a whiteboard in the conference room where we meet to evaluate their sketches on the first day.

10 Rules of Sketching

In the same email, I attach a slideshow that goes over the **10 Rules of Sketching**, which were described in Chapter 3. These rules are listed below:

1. Sketch a wireframe.

2. Draw one concept per page.

3. Do not use special paper.

4. Use black markers on white paper.

5. Do not use a computer for sketching.

6. Do not color sketches.

7. Use a title and description.

8. Use annotations to provide clarity.

9. Use arrows to show interactions.

10. Use sticky notes sparingly.

You can download the slides from the companion website for this book: http://www.designstudiomethod.com.

How Many Sketches Should Each Person Draw Initially?

Initially, Sketchers should produce five or six high-level design concepts. In my experience, your participants need to generate about 20–30 initial sketches. These sketches should be completely different concepts, not slightly different variations of the same general idea. The Sketcher's goal is to generate and explore alternatives. The Sketchers should challenge themselves. You do not want Sketchers to just refine a concept or risk getting committed to a single idea. Leaders want to force participants to engage their imagination to come up with something new and innovative. In my experience, five or six sketches get most people out of the common response zone. Innovative products are not produced in the common response zone.

TIP #1:

Participants should initially create five or six sketches alone.

How Many Sketches Does the Group Need Initially?

As a team, the entire group needs to generate 20–30 sketches to ensure the team gets out of the common response zone. When you have a cross-functional team of five or six sketchers, you should be able to reach 20–30 sketches easily.

The sketches must be unique. If someone produces variations of the same basic concept, it is both non-productive and counter-productive. By sketching the same basic concept, a person is either thinking too much about one idea or not enough about other ideas. The danger is how **counter-productive** it can be to sketch the same basic concept. When people focus on a single concept in the early rounds of a design studio, you risk encountering:

- **An Escalation of Commitment.** When someone spends a lot of time on an idea, they become more committed to it. By sketching the same basic concept, a Sketcher runs the risk of getting committed to it without seeing the sketches of other participants.

- **Staying in the Common Response Zone.** By not producing unique sketches, your Sketchers run the risk of staying in the common response zone. Innovation does not occur in the common response zone.

- **Fixating on a Single Concept Too Early.** The first rule of generating ideas is that quantity leads to quality, as described in Chapter 2. By iterating on the same concept, you may not have enough sketches to find a quality idea.

Do not allow participants to sketch the same basic idea.

When someone does not produce five or six unique sketches, it might be a confidence or respect issue. You will have participants who do not feel comfortable sketching and presenting their ideas. Other participants will be very intimidated by the entire process. In these situations, it is a confidence issue. Your participants will let you know, too. If they put forth their best effort and do not draw enough sketches (but really tried), you have willing participants doing their best in a design studio.

In other cases, you will encounter respect issues with some participants. They may not want to participate in sketching. Some people may actually want to damage the output from a design studio based on a hidden agenda or political objective. In these instances, it is a respect issue. They do not respect the process or the people. As described in this book, the design studio method reflects over 100 years of creative problem-solving research. The other participants have scheduled their valuable time to generate and evaluate ideas. If you encounter a respect issue, talk with the person. If needed, dismiss them from participating with the other Sketchers.

In some cases, a person may not understand the importance of sketching five to six unique ideas. When this happens, you need to explain the reason

TIP #2:

As a team, the goal is 20–30 sketches for the first round.

TIP #3:

Sketches must be unique, especially in the first round.

for sketching a certain number of unique ideas. You must let them know it is a respect issue. I tell the group to take a break. As discreetly as possible, I ask this person to come with me for a private conversation. After a brief chat, I give this participant 20–30 minutes to do their work. To show respect to my chastised participant, I return to the group to let them know we will have a slight delay for an important phone call. This delay gives the other participant time to complete their sketches.

Unfortunately, if someone continues to not perform or resists participating with the group, I excuse them from the design studio. At this point, my decision is non-negotiable.

It is a respect issue.

The 5-3-1 Sketching Formula

Based upon my experience, I have developed a 5-3-1 sketching formula to determine the number of sketches needed for most design studios. For most problems, you will need two or three rounds of sketching before you can mash up the final design concept on a whiteboard. The following table illustrates the number of sketches that must be produced per round for a design studio with six participants.

Design Studio Round	# of Participants	# of Sketches per Person	Total # of Sketches
First Round	6	5	30
Second Round	6	3	18
Final Round	6	1	6

Let's look at how the 5-3-1 formula typically works in a design studio. In the first round, participants show their sketches to the rest of the team. The Sketchers will evaluate each of the ideas by using positive judgment first. Then, they critically evaluate each sketch. At the end of the first round the Sketchers vote on the most popular ideas. Participants will see different ideas in the first round. They will re-sketch three ideas for the second round.

You should give participants 30–45 minutes to sketch between the first and second round. The Sketchers will merge popular design elements from the 25–30 sketches shown in the first round into their three sketches for the second round. In some cases, a participant will completely abandon their design ideas to create an amalgamation of the different design elements from other people. You will also see people who tweak one of their initial sketches with some design elements shown in another person's sketch. The second round is a critical step, where you start to see people converging on specific design elements.

SEVERAL OPPORTUNITIES EXIST TO GENERATE AND EVALUATE IDEAS

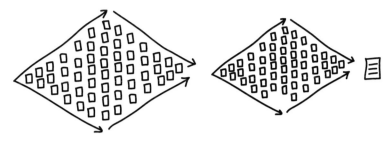

Sketchers use positive judgment first to evaluate the sketches, followed by a critical inspection, and voting in the second round. The participants must produce one final sketch for the final round. Typically, I give them 20 minutes. In addition, I ask them to produce a very detailed sketch.

In the final round, you will have six sketches from six participants. I typically hang the sketches side-by-side to make it easy for people to make comparisons. Each person describes their final sketch for about five minutes. We will quickly evaluate the positive and negative aspects of each design. Then, we do our final vote. In most cases, you will see participants focus on two or three designs, which we use for mashing up the team's final concept on the whiteboard.

TIP #4:

Use the 5-3-1 model to know how many sketches to produce.

DESIGN LIKE DA VINCI: SKETCHING WAS HIS GREATEST LEGACY

In his lifetime, Leonardo da Vinci produced over 13,000 pages of sketches. Within his sketchbooks, Leonardo thinks scientifically and creatively. You can find sketches of futuristic devices, detailed drawings of human anatomy, postulations on plate tectonics, observations about diet, exercise, and heart disease. You can find sketches of weapons, flowers, soldiers, flying machines, horses, and more. Some sketches serve as wireframes for statues and bridges, while other are early renditions of paintings. For da Vinci, his sketches were his visual thoughts.

Thirteen thousand pages of sketches is a large number. If you were to read 13,000 pages, you could read the following books:

Harry Potter Series	4,100
+ Chronicles of Narnia	768
+ Lord of the Rings Trilogy	1,011
+ Hunger Games Trilogy	1,155
+ Game of Thrones Series	4,197
+ 9/11 Commission Report	1,181
+ NIV Bible	585
TOTAL PAGES	12,997

Leonardo da Vinci was the archetype of a Renaissance man—artist, mathematician, sculptor, scientist, writer, and more. As an artist, Leonardo produced a very small sample of great work that included the Mona Lisa and The Last Supper. *Leonardo was a prolific sketcher, and his 13,000 pages are arguably his greatest legacy.*

Avoiding Groupthink

Groupthink is a psychological phenomenon that occurs within a group of people, where a desire for group harmony in decision-making overrides the realistic appraisal of alternatives. The design studio method provides several mechanisms to specifically avoid groupthink:

- Sketchers initially produce concepts alone. They do not collaborate with others.
- The Leader and Historian do not generate or evaluate concepts.
- Only a Sketcher evaluates concepts, which allows them to freely express doubts.
- The Leader avoids contact with Sketchers to avoid influencing an outcome.
- Sketchers can collaborate with their teammates outside of the design studio. A word of caution: You do not want two sketchers to collaborate with the same teammate. It gives this person too much influence in the design studio.
- All sketches should be examined for positive and negative values.
- Sketchers can discuss the group's ideas with trusted people outside of the group.
- Sketchers can discuss and ask questions of experts (watch for undue influence).
- Group discussions use Edward de Bono's Six Thinking Hats method.

The first rule to avoid groupthink is to initially sketch alone.

TIP #5:

Design studios have many built-in mechanisms to avoid groupthink.

PROJECT SPOTLIGHT: WORLD USABILITY DAY WIDGET

In the last chapter, the design studio team started to conduct user and design research to better understand about switching from an incandescent to an LED bulb. Two participants talked with some construction workers and visited a local hardware store. They returned from the hardware store with literature from lighting manufacturers. Meanwhile, their teammates performed design research by doing several Internet searches. They visited the Energy Star site and several light bulb manufacturing sites to determine energy and cost savings. The graphic designers decided to look at how sites were designed for comparison shopping.

The next step was to sketch separately.

Each person was given 30 minutes to produce five sketches. The Group Leader instructed the participants to sketch alone. Several participants sketched more than five sketches. As it turns out, one Sketcher would produce four sketches, which were slight tweaks of the same concept. The Leader gently reminded this Sketcher of the importance of making the sketches unique. He was given another 15 minutes to come up with some unique sketches.

He came back with seven sketches! The Sketcher simply needed to be challenged.

Summary

- Before they start sketching, remind participants about:
  - o Four Rules for Generating Ideas (Chapter 2)
  - o 10 Rules of Sketching (Chapter 3)
- To ensure individual creativity, people should initially sketch alone.
- Each person should create five or six unique sketches.
- If a person does not produce five or six sketches, they are non-productive.
- If a person does not produce unique sketches, they are counter-productive.
- Unique sketches are important because:
  - o They get you out of the common response zone.
  - o Quantity leads to quality.
  - o They reduce the chance of an escalation of commitment.
- As a team, your project needs 25–30 sketches for each problem on the first day.
- The 5-3-1 model shows the number of sketches each person should sketch per round.
- The design studio method has many built-in mechanisms to avoid groupthink.

CHAPTER 12

Evaluating Sketches as a Team

The success of any design studio depends upon people's ability to generate and evaluate sketches. In some respects, generating sketches is easier than evaluating them. After reflecting upon user and design research, a person sketches new ideas based on what they have learned. While sketching is an individual act, evaluation is a group activity. Luckily, the Six Thinking Hats provide you with a very effective communication tool to help participants evaluate the sketches. The ordering of the hats helps you steer the group's discussion. In this chapter, you will learn a step-by-step approach to help you with evaluating sketches.

"True genius resides in the capacity for evaluation of uncertain, hazardous, and conflicting information."
– Winston Churchill

Draw a Design Studios Processes Sketch

Before your design studio participants arrive, you should draw a "Design Studio Processes" sketch for people to review. When they arrive, you can quickly review the processes to set expectations, remind participants, and reinforce the processes for new participants.

You will be surprised at how often people refer to this sketch throughout your design studio.

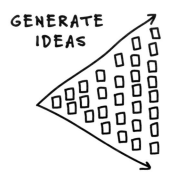
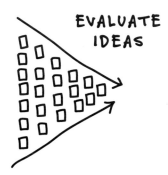

GENERATE IDEAS	EVALUATE IDEAS
1. Strive for Quantity	1. Use Positive Judgment
2. Defer Judgment	2. Consider Novelty
3. Seek New Combinations	3. Narrow Deliberately
4. Use Your Imagination	4. Stay on Course

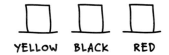

BLUE   WHITE   GREEN   YELLOW   BLACK   RED

Supplies You Will Need for the Group

Once your participants come together to evaluate sketches, participants will hang, group, move, re-group, review, rank, vote, and take pictures of the sketches. Stock these supplies to make the process of evaluating sketches easier for your participants:

- **Paper.** People will sketch, doodle, write, and vote on paper.
- **Markers.** Use fat-nib, black markers on white paper for maximum contrast.
- **Tape.** Masking tape works fine. People will be moving their sketches.
- **Whiteboard.** Use a whiteboard to mash up the final sketches.
- **Wash Cloths.** You should wash the whiteboard after using it.
- **Dot Stickers.** Some people like to use dot stickers for public voting.
- **File Folders.** Store the paper sketches in the file folders.
- **Hand Sanitizer.** Markers are messy, especially in a design studio.
- **Camera.** Take pictures with a smart phone or camera.

- **Butcher Paper.** You can tape the sketches to butcher paper and roll them up.

If you accidentally use a permanent marker on a whiteboard, do not worry. Before the permanent marker dries, trace over it with a washable marker. The ink blends, and then you can wipe it off. I recommend washing the whiteboard, too.

Ways to Avoid Groupthink during Group Evaluation

Group evaluation does not have to be groupthink.

The primary purpose of the evaluation is to have a realistic appraisal of alternatives. People should have open, frank conversations rather than trying to maintain group harmony (or groupthink). When you do evaluate the sketches, it should be a structured discussion between team members. It should not be a test of someone's persuasive abilities or validation of a hidden agenda. Follow these guidelines to ensure your participants more effectively evaluate concepts:

- Do not do problem-solving when you evaluate sketches.
- Evaluating sketches is a time to clarify and analyze the proposed solutions.
- Each concept is presented by the person who created it.
- Participants should present their ideas as if someone else sketched it.
- Ask clarifying questions before critiquing, such as the design intent of the sketcher.
- Only the Sketchers can evaluate the designs of other Sketchers.
- The Leader guides the discussion and does not participate in the evaluations.
- Review the positive benefits of sketches before critically evaluating them.
- No voting occurs until all ideas have been evaluated.

You will see how each of these guidelines is used throughout the rest of this chapter.

STEP #1: REVIEW AND PREVIEW

Before the Sketchers show their work, the Leader should set expectations, build rapport, and set the tone with participants. As mentioned earlier, the Leader will already have sketched the different processes that will be used in the design studio. The Leader should review the four rules of creative thinking, four rules of critical thinking, Six Thinking Hats, and six fundamentals of sketching. The Leader should answer any questions before continuing with the design studio. Based upon my experience, this initial review establishes the Leader's authority with the team.

After describing the design studio processes, the Leader should preview how the Six Thinking Hats will be used in a specific order. For the sake of clarity, I walk the participants through an example with one sketch. You want participants to get familiar with using the hats, especially the ordering. I will refer participants to the process drawings of the rules and hats before I do my explanation. Here is an example of the dialogue that I usually say:

> Each hat represents a different way of thinking. As the Leader, I wear the blue hat, which is the organizing hat. Your sketches represent the green hat, which is the creative hat. When you present your sketches, you should wear the white hat, which is about facts. You should tell us how a customer might use your design. We use positive judgment first to evaluate a sketch, which is the yellow hat. After all of the green-hat sketches have been evaluated using the yellow hat, we will use the black hat to do a critical inspection of a potential green-hat idea. After we review all of the sketches for both yellow-hat and black-hat comments, we will use the red hat, which is the emotional hat used for voting. When you finally make a decision, it will be based upon your own knowledge, experience, and intuition. All the sketches were presented and evaluated to lead up to your red-hat vote. We will use the hats throughout the process. If you forget the meaning of a hat, you can look at the sketch on the whiteboard. Within a few hours, the Six Thinking Hats will be like an old hat. They will be comfortable to use in your daily conversations.

Within a few hours, all of the participants are using the Six Thinking Hats. Plus, they refer to the sketch of the design studio processes to anticipate the next step.

STEP #2: ASK PARTICIPANTS ABOUT STRUGGLE POINTS

Before showing any of the initial sketches, you may want to ask participants to tell you about any areas where they struggled. As the Sketchers talk about their struggles, they build a natural rapport and bond with the other participants. In some cases, the participants may work on the same team, but they do not work together on a daily basis. In addition, the struggle points of the Sketcher may end up being the exact same issues your customers encounter.

Several years ago, I was conducting a design studio with a group of people who worked in different parts of the globe. They talked on the phone and used chat software on a daily basis. Two people had a natural animosity because of their job roles and their past experiences with each other. When I asked them about struggle points, these two people regularly experienced problems with the same issues: overcoming the current state of the product, screen real estate, and fear of rejection.

I said, "Welcome to the world of design!"

These two people bonded in a tremendous way during the next few days. One participant told me the initial question on struggle points helped him to realize he had always been working to solve the same problem differently. His co-worker agreed. A bond was created.

They are still friends and co-workers today.

STEP #3: SHOWING EACH SKETCH

When someone shows their sketch, they tape it to a wall, where everyone else can see it. While explaining a sketch, the presenter uses white-hat thinking to show how a customer might use the design. The Historian takes a picture of each sketch. An example appears below.

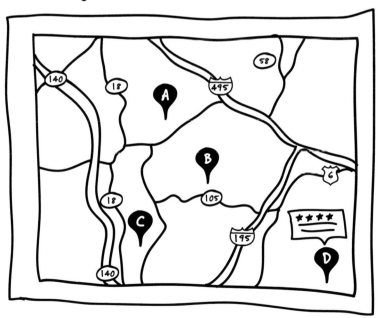

The primary purpose of the above sketch is to search for available hotels on a phone. The explanation should be very straightforward. If someone uses white-hat thinking, the explanation focuses on the features and functionality of the design. You might hear this type of white-hat explanation:

"In portrait mode, the phone displays a list of hotels for the customer to choose. A filter can be used for preferred hotels, when customers belong to a loyalty program. If the customer rotates their phone, the list of hotels shows up in a map view. Customers can select a hotel from the map to get a better description of it."

When participants use white-hat thinking, the explanation of a sketch is short and concise.

It is about facts.

When a participant becomes emotionally attached to their sketch, their description resembles either self-praise or self-criticism. When someone really likes their design, you might hear this type of self-praise (or lobbying):

"I worked extremely hard on this design. I spent hours and hours on it. The list view of the hotels is pretty standard, but I added this cool feature where people could filter, because we all know people belong to a hotel rewards program. But, the really cool feature is when they rotate the phone and it becomes a map. I showed this sketch to the marketing team and they love it!"

The explanation is long and full of self-praise. This person is wearing the yellow hat. Ask them to wear the white hat.

When someone doubts their design, their description can be full of self-criticism. You might hear this type of explanation about the hotel sketch:

"I really struggled with this design. I am not sure you are going to like it. The list view is very standard. You have probably seen a hundred designs like it. I went and added a different view when you rotate the phone, but I think our customers will not like it. There is not a button to click right away on the map view. I think it is confusing."

In this case, the explanation is long and full of self-criticism. This person is wearing the black hat. Ask them to wear the white hat.

Participants should present their idea as if someone else sketched it. They should remove all emotion from the presentation of the sketch. Plus, the positive and negative evaluation of the sketches will be a group activity. It is not a public display of self-aggrandizement or humiliation. It is about the sketch, not the person.

Plus, it really saves a lot of time.

STEP #4: ASKING CLARIFYING QUESTIONS

After initially seeing an individual sketch, participants can ask clarifying questions on how a specific design works. **Clarifying questions help your participants to perform better critiques.** Participants should be reminded to defer judgment, which is the first rule of evaluating sketches. Instead, you want to hear questions about:

TIP #1:

Participants should present the idea as if someone else sketched it. In this approach, a person just explains the features and functions of a sketch. You might hear this type of explanation:

"In this design, the customer turns their phone to see a map view. The map view shows information based upon their search results. The hotel maps have pin points to show their exact location in the city. The customer can select a hotel pin to view more information, such as star ratings and amenities. If desired, the customer can select a hotel to complete their booking or they can rotate their phone to get the list view of their search results."

By presenting the sketch in a neutral way, you do not see a public display of self-aggrandizement or humiliation. It is about the sketch, not the person.

Plus, it really saves a lot of time.

"Simplicity is the ultimate sophistication."
– Leonardo da Vinci

- **Design Intent.** Participants ask these questions to determine the problem(s) the designer was trying to solve in their sketch.
- **Design Execution.** Participants ask these questions to determine the form and functional elements of a design.

In this respect, you want to hear white-hat questions asked to the presenter of each sketch. It really saves time and focuses the conversation. By asking clarifying questions about design intent and execution, your participants will be able to better critique a design, because they more fully understand the sketch and the problem someone is trying to solve.

During the evaluation phase, the best insights come from the questions asked about the designer's intent. Questions about design intent are really asking a profound, design question: What problem are you trying to solve with this design? The answers to design-intent questions focus the participants to do more problem-solving and less criticizing.

DESIGN-INTENT QUESTIONS YOU MIGHT HEAR:

- *What problem is this design trying to resolve?*
- *Are there any other problems you are trying to solve?*
- *How does this design solve our main problem?*
- *What was your intent with this specific feature?*
- *Can you describe the step-by-step outcomes as a customer uses this design?*

While design-intent questions focus on the problem(s), design-execution questions focus on a solution's implementation, or how a sketch solves the problem. When you evaluate a sketch's execution, you want to look at its form and function:

- **Form.** The form of a design refers to its visual qualities, or aesthetics. The layout, icons, color, and typography are some of the elements of form.
- **Function.** The functional elements of a design refer to its ability to solve a problem, such as navigation, learnability, ease of use, findability, readability, and so on.

In other words, design-execution questions ask how a design solves a problem, and design-intent questions ask why a designer sketched their drawing (i.e., their motivation or inspiration).

DESIGN-EXECUTION QUESTIONS YOU MIGHT HEAR:

- *What usability issues does this sketch solve?*
- *What is the primary purpose of this feature? Page? Design element?*
- *Why did you place the data in this order?*
- *What was your reason(s) for choosing this layout?*
- *Can you explain the navigation in this sketch?*

TIP #2:

When they see a sketch, people can ask about design intent and execution.

After each sketch is presented, participants can ask clarifying questions on design intent and design execution only. Participants should not express positive and negative comments as sketches are presented. Positive and negative judgments come after grouping the sketches.

STEP #5: GROUPING THE SKETCHES

After taping, presenting, and answering questions about their sketches, your participants will see a series of sketches on the wall. Many of the sketches will contain similar design elements. The Leader should have participants group similar concepts together. During this exercise, the Leader and Historian should not participate in the grouping exercise. Instead, the Leader and Historian should listen carefully to how the Sketchers classify their sketches.

TIP #3:

After presenting all of the sketches, the participants should group them.

The illustration below left shows 20 different sketches that were created for an actual design studio. At a quick glance, you may notice that some sketches look alike.

The participants worked together to cluster similar-looking sketches as a team. The illustration below right shows how the participants clustered the sketches together.

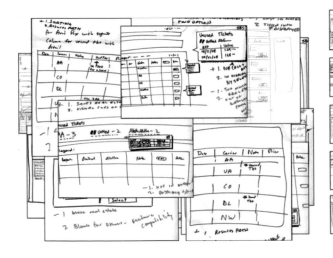

As you can see, four main clusters emerged. The Leader and Historian silently listened to the team's conversation for insights on the team's initial thinking. The team would decide upon a name for each cluster and write it above the top sketch in the cluster. The Historian takes a picture of the clusters and stores it in a common location.

TIP #4:

Grouping the sketches provides initial insights into the thoughts of the team.

STEP #6: EVALUATE EACH SKETCH POSITIVELY

In this step, participants need to look at each sketch individually to explore the positive values and benefits of a potential idea. The Leader should reiterate lessons from earlier in the book:

- Use positive judgment first when you evaluate ideas.
- In some cases, you must consider the novelty of an idea.
- Some ideas need to be further developed.
- The yellow hat explores the positive aspects of a green-hat sketch.
- Some sketches will lead to inspiration for another person.

Let's explore the value and benefit of the mobile phone sketch, which is shown below.

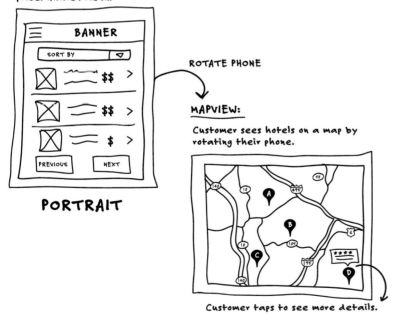

LISTVIEW:

Customer can sort. They see hotels from lowest to highest price. Hidden menu.

BANNER

SORT BY

$$ >
$$ >
$ >

PREVIOUS   NEXT

PORTRAIT

ROTATE PHONE

MAPVIEW:

Customer sees hotels on a map by rotating their phone.

Customer taps to see more details.

LANDSCAPE

Rather than deliberating on designs, ask participants for two or three positive comments for each sketch. The natural process of evaluating, voting, re-sketching, and mashing up ensures the participants will rally around the best design elements. Three positive comments for this sketch might be:

- The layout of the portrait view has a nice flow with picture, description, and prices.
- The pictures in portrait view help with brand reinforcement.
- Rotating between list and map view is a natural interaction on a smartphone.

After the participants give two or three positive comments, you go to another sketch for more positive comments until all the sketches are reviewed for positive values and benefits.

TIP #5:

Give positive comments to every sketch before evaluating them critically.

STEP #7: EVALUATE CRITICALLY

After you have viewed all the sketches using positive judgment first, you should critically evaluate each one. You may want to explain to participants that they should limit emotional responses at this point. As mentioned earlier, the process of evaluating, voting, re-sketching, and mashing up ensures the participants will rally around the best design elements. Plus, emotional feelings can be expressed best by not voting on a specific design.

Before making their negative criticism of a design, encourage participants to ask themselves these types of questions:

- Does this design actually solve your problem?
- Is this the best solution? What is not developed enough?
- What technical problems exist? Is it even feasible?
- How does this concept impact other products?
- Is the execution wrong? (example: incorrect form and function)
- Does this solve one problem, but create another one?

You should encourage participants to think about their positive and negative comments. By asking these questions before responding, the critical comments are more thoughtful and less emotional.

Let's critically explore the mobile app to determine three negative comments.

As with the positive comments, limit the negative comments to two or three observations. For the mobile app, you might hear these three negative comments:

- On the portrait view, the banner seems to be too large. Screen real estate is valuable.
- On the portrait view, more hotels may be listed, but the buttons act as a scroll stopper.
- Additional features seem to be hidden in both views. Customers might miss them.

Other negative comments may exist, but voting (or not voting) for a sketch is the ultimate comment.

STEP #8: DETERMINE COMMON THEMES

After you have inspected each sketch for positive and negative attributes, you should review all of the sketches for common themes. On the surface, the natural groupings are easy to see because the team clustered the sketches together. The Leader should ask these questions:

- What are common things you see within each grouping?
- What are common things you see in different categories?
- What design elements do you see repeated in all of the sketches?
- What are the most popular design elements?
- Why do you think these design elements are important?

The Leader just writes down a bulleted list to capture the common elements based upon the group's evaluation. The Historian takes a picture of this list to store in a common location.

Evaluating Sketches in the Final Round

You may want to evaluate your sketches differently in the final round. In the early rounds, you need to have people quickly present, cluster similar sketches, evaluate positively, analyze critically, and vote. With so many sketches and a set amount of time, you must work quickly and efficiently. In the final round, you want your participants to pause and reflect when they evaluate the sketches. In the final round, I have participants use a **1-2-1** evaluation.

A **1-2-1** evaluation approach is a popular critiquing style in art and design schools. In this approach, your critique begins and ends with positive comments:

- 1 positive comment about the sketch
- 2 critical comments about the sketch
- 1 positive comment about the sketch

For me, the last round is an ideal place to do a **1-2-1 critique**.

In the final round, each participant shows only one sketch. You do not need to cluster because each sketch should be evaluated independently. Participants have already invested a lot of time on their different ideas, so you might start to have an escalation of commitment happening. The simple act of changing the evaluation method to a 1-2-1 critique helps participants to re-focus. Plus, it helps to soften any negative comments that might be viewed as criticism, by putting critical comments between two positive ones.

A 1-2-1 critique is a simple, powerful tool.

> **TIP #6:**
>
> *You may want to use a 1-2-1 critique in the final round because your participants have been working very hard.*

PROJECT SPOTLIGHT: WORLD USABILITY DAY WIDGET

In the last chapter, we learned how the different teams had shared their user and design research with the other people in their group. Each team was given 30 minutes to produce five or six sketches. Participants were told to sketch alone. Some people began sketching right away. Other participants performed additional research. After 30 minutes, they gathered with their team to begin the process of evaluating the sketches.

My friend, Cone Johnson, and I made sure each team had tape, paper, and markers. We gave these instructions to the teams:

1. Spend one minute explaining each of the sketches.

2. Ask questions about design intent or execution.

3. Defer judgment (both positive and negative).

4. After each sketch is presented, cluster them into groups.

5. Name each group.

6. For each sketch, give two or three positive comments. Do not give negative comments.

7. After giving positive comments for all sketches, give two or three negative comments.

8. Write down common themes on a separate sheet of paper.

The teams were given 60 minutes to complete the evaluation of the sketches.

As the teams were talking about their sketches, I reminded them of the Six Thinking Hats and the four rules for evaluating ideas (use positive judgment first, consider novelty, be deliberate when narrowing options, and stay on course). Participants liked the interactivity—presenting, asking questions, seeing other sketches, evaluating, and talking.

The evaluation process was engaging, enjoyable, and exhausting. Our cross-functional team saw incredible results. The participants:

- Produced 32 individual sketches.

- Clustered the sketches into five groups.

- Found 72 positive comments for all of the sketches.

- Found 76 critical comments for all of the sketches.

- Uncovered 12 common themes in their sketches.

In this final round, we did a 1-2-1 critique of the final sketches.

The team was ready to vote on their sketches, which is our next chapter.

Summary

- Draw a Design Studio Process sketch before participants arrive.
- Stock your room with paper, markers, and other supplies people may need.
- Review the Design Studio Process sketch when participants arrive.
- Group evaluation is not the same thing as groupthink.
- The design studio has many built-in mechanisms to prevent groupthink.
- The steps for evaluating sketches include:
  - o **Step #1:** Review design studio processes. Preview the evaluation steps by using a random example.
  - o **Step #2:** Ask the Sketchers about their struggle points, to build team chemistry. Plus, you may reveal design constraints and uncover potential customer issues.
  - o **Step #3:** Sketchers present their designs by explaining how a customer might use it. While presenting, the Sketcher can act like another person produced the sketch.
  - o **Step #4:** After a sketch is presented, people ask clarifying questions about design intent and execution. They should defer judgment. The Historian takes a picture.
  - o **Step #5:** After all sketches are presented, the team clusters them into groups. Pay attention to the conversation. The Historian takes a picture of the clusters.
  - o **Step #6:** Evaluate all of the sketches for their positive aspects. Two or three comments per sketch are enough. Do not give negative comments at this time.
  - o **Step #7:** Evaluate all of the sketches critically. Two or three negative comments are enough. Do not give negative comments at the same time as positive ones.
  - o **Step #8:** Ask participants to review the sketches for common themes. It is a great way to wrap up the evaluation phase. The Historian can take a picture of the common themes.
- In the final round, consider a **1-2-1** critique:
  - o One positive comment, two critical ones, and one positive comment.
  - o The 1-2-1 approach is a proven critiquing method in art and design schools.
  - o It is a simple way to re-focus a group.
  - o A 1-2-1 critique softens any negative comments that might be seen as criticism.

CHAPTER 13

Voting on the Best Ideas

Every vote counts in a design studio. Voting is important, because it is how your participants make decisions about what they see. In the end, a person's vote will be based upon their experience, knowledge, and intuition. You really do not know if the team's decision on a final concept will be accepted by your customers.

Voting is, literally, a leap of faith.

"Thinking isn't agreeing or disagreeing. That's voting."
– Robert Frost

Voting can be very difficult for participants. In the later rounds, you will see many of the sketches as viable options.

Since the Sketchers produce the work, they have a vested interest in the final result. So, only Sketchers can vote. The Leader explains the voting process. The Leader does not vote. The Leader and Historian tally votes, acting as impartial witnesses to the group's decision.

SEVERAL OPPORTUNITIES EXIST TO GENERATE AND EVALUATE IDEAS

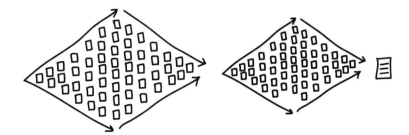

The 20% Rule

As described in Chapter 11, the **5-3-1** sketching formula determines the number of sketches needed for most design studios. The following table shows the number of sketches produced per round for a design studio with six participants.

Round	# of Participants	# of Sketches/Person	Total # of Sketches
First Round	6	5	30
Second Round	6	3	18
Final Round	6	1	6

When the Sketchers vote in the different rounds, I have adopted a **20% rule** based upon the number of total sketches. As shown below, participants will cast several votes in each round.

Round	# of Participants	# of Sketches/ Person	Total # of Sketches	20% Rule
First Round	6	5	30	6
Second Round	6	3	18	4
Final Round	6	1	6	2

For the rest of the chapter, you will see how the 20% rule works in each round.

Voting Procedures in Round 1

For the sake of clarity, let's use the example from the above table, where six participants created five sketches each for a total of 30 designs. Participants will present, answer questions, and group sketches. After grouping them, participants will evaluate the 30 sketches with 60–90 positive and negative comments total. Common themes would be explored in a group discussion.

Finally, it is time to vote.

Before participants cast their votes, the Leader must explain the voting process. Based upon my experience, a public discussion where people lobby for their favorite designs leads to groupthink and gridlock in the decision-making process. Besides, public deliberation has already occurred when participants evaluated the sketches for their positive and negative aspects. Instead, participants will perform a public vote with little, or no, discussion. When it is time to vote, the participants cast their votes.

When it is time to vote, you may want to use these voting guidelines in Round 1:

- **20% Rule:** The number of votes is based on 20% of the total number of sketches. For example, 30 total sketches would mean each participant receives 6 votes.

- **No Person Can Stuff the Ballot:** Each participant may vote on a particular sketch only one time. For example, a person cannot cast all six votes for the same sketch.

- **Several People Can Vote on the Same Sketch.** Each person can cast a single vote on the same sketch. With six people, a sketch can have a maximum of six votes.

- **Vote on the Sketch:** Each person should vote on the sketch to get an accurate record. Dot voting or checkmarks can be used. In other words, do not vote on the whiteboard.

- **No Voting Blocks.** Participants are discouraged from forming voting blocks. The voting should occur quickly with little talking.

- **Public Voting:** Each participant will be voting in public. Participants can all go at the same time. No deliberation is needed, as they have already evaluated the sketches.

The Historian takes a picture of the sketches that received a vote.

After presenting, grouping, evaluating, and voting, everyone will be exhausted. The Leader should tell participants to take a break, eat lunch, or drink some coffee. The Sketchers should be given 30–60 minutes to sketch new concepts based upon what they have seen in the design studio. Plus, they should be reminded of the sketches that received a vote and the common themes people saw in the sketches.

Voting Procedures in Round 2

Continuing with the same example, six participants will create three sketches each, for a total of 18 designs in the second round. Again, the participants will present, answer questions, and group sketches. After grouping them, participants will evaluate the 18 sketches with 36–48 positive and negative comments total. Common themes can be explored in a group discussion.

In the second round, you use the same voting procedures that were used in Round 1. The sketches will be more developed, as participants have combined some of the best design elements into their sketches. With more developed sketches, the voting becomes much harder for the Sketchers. After the participants finish voting, the Historian takes a picture of the sketches that receive a vote.

The Leader gives the participants 30 minutes to produce a final sketch. The Sketchers are reminded of the votes and the common themes seen in the sketches. The final round begins.

Voting Procedures in the Final Round

TIP #3:

People love to vote for their own sketches. Use ranking to determine the most popular alternatives.

In the final round, each person will produce one sketch. With six participants, you will see six sketches. When it is time to vote, use these voting guidelines for the final round:

- **A Label for Each Design.** The Leader will label the five or six remaining designs. Participants will use this label when they vote.
- **Rank the Top Two Designs.** People rank the top two designs. Most people will vote on their own idea. You need to know everyone's second favorite design.
- **Provide an Explanation.** After ranking each idea, participants will write out the reason for their vote. The Leader will read the explanation to the group.
- **Private Voting.** Each participant is given a sheet of paper to rank their top two choices and provide their explanation. Voting sheets are given to the Leader.
- **Tallying Votes.** The Leader will read each of the votes out loud. The number will be tallied next to each design label.

By ranking the sketches, you can determine the most popular designs to merge (or mash up) in the final mockup.

How to Analyze the Votes in the Final Round

Since people rank their top two choices, you will receive some different insights. People must weigh two options. Participants will be writing out the reasons for their choices. When you evaluate how the votes were cast, you can analyze the first and second choices in several ways:

1. Which sketch received the most #1 votes?
2. Which sketch received the most overall votes?
3. Did any of the designs receive the same number of votes?
4. Which designs did not receive any votes?
5. Could any designs be merged?
6. Did two similar-looking designs split the votes?

In one design studio, one design received the most #1 votes. Yet, another design received the most overall votes, with every participant casting one vote on this design. The design with the most votes became the main design used in the final mockup created on the whiteboard.

PROJECT SPOTLIGHT: WORLD USABILITY DAY WIDGET

In the last chapter, we learned that our cross-functional team had generated and evaluated many concepts for the widget to swap an incandescent bulb for an LED bulb. They had:

- Produced 32 individual sketches.
- Clustered the sketches into five groups.
- Found 72 positive comments for all of the sketches.
- Found 76 critical comments for all of the sketches.
- Uncovered 12 common themes in their sketches.

With 32 sketches, participants had six votes to cast in the first round.

The participants cast their votes directly on the sketches by placing checkmarks on their preferred sketches. Five sketches received four or more votes. You could find other sketches with either one or two votes each. Many sketches received no votes.

Based upon their analysis, the participants decided to do a second round of sketching. In the second round, the participants decided to do just two sketches because the votes were being cast on five main sketches.

They were given 20 minutes to do their sketches.

In the second round, the participants returned with 10 sketches. They evaluated the sketches and gave two positive and two critical comments for each sketch. Some of the sketches were virtually identical, so the participants decided to group them together by covering up a sketch. After reducing their sketches, the team had only six sketches.

Using the 20% rule, each participant was given two votes to cast. I suggested using a private vote, where they ranked their two most preferred designs with a brief explanation of their voting choice. After tallying the votes, two designs emerged with all of the votes.

It was time to move to the next step to create a final mockup. We will review this step in the next chapter.

Summary

- Voting is based on a person's knowledge, experience, and intuition.
- Voting is a leap of faith.
- There are two voting principles in a design studio:
  - o Only Sketchers can vote, as they have a vested interest.
  - o The Leader and Historian tally votes and act as witnesses.
- Use the 20% rule to determine the number of votes in any given sketching round (e.g., 30 sketches equals six votes).
- Early-round voting should be done in public.
- Early-round voting guidelines include:
  - o No person can spend all of their votes on one sketch.
  - o Several people can (and should) vote on the same sketch, if desired.
  - o Participants should mark their vote on the sketch itself to keep a permanent record.
  - o People should not form voting blocks.
  - o Public voting is usually done in the early rounds to help with conversations.
  - o People should not try to sway voters to their designs.
- Last-round voting guidelines include:
  - o The Leader provides a label for each design.
  - o Participants vote privately, where they rank the final sketches.
  - o Participants should write the name of the sketch, rank, and an explanation.
  - o The explanation should describe the reason(s) for ranking each design.
  - o Votes are handed to the Leader, who tallies them up.
  - o The Leader reads how each person ranked the designs and their reason(s).
  - o As a team, the group analyzes how everyone voted.

CHAPTER 14

Producing a Final Mockup

After casting their votes in the final round of a design studio, participants will need to combine two or three sketches into a final mockup. The process of merging sketches together is known as mashing up. It differs from other sketching activities in two significant ways:

1. Mashing up is a group sketching activity rather than an individual process.

2. The final mockup is sketched on a whiteboard, not paper.

All participants should talk about the design elements openly, while one person sketches the final mockup on the whiteboard. Since the final mockup is constantly tweaked during the mashup, a whiteboard rather than paper is the best surface on which to produce this group sketch.

"Finishing is better than starting."
– Ecclesiastes 7:8

STEP #8: MASHUP

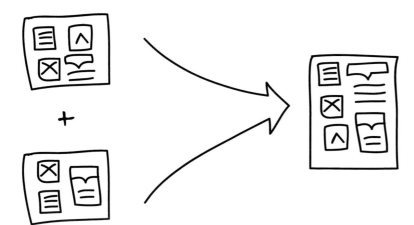

The easiest way to explain a mashup is to show how the World Usability Day widget was done.

PROJECT SPOTLIGHT: WORLD USABILITY DAY WIDGET

Participants were given a task to create a widget for the World Usability Day home page.

World Usability Day

For that year, the theme for World Usability Day was sustainability. The widget would be placed on the site to entice consumers to switch from an incandescent bulb to an LED. Participants were given a minimal amount of information, including this table from a light bulb manufacturer:

	Standard	LED
Bulb Power	50 watts	4.2 watts
Initial Price	$2.00	$42.50
KwH per Year	146	32
Yearly Operating Costs	$15.50	$3.25
Lifetime of Bulbs (Hours)	715	5000
Total Dollar Costs	$197.50	$85.00
Total Energy Used	250,000	21,000

As described earlier, the sketching activities occurred this way:

- Round 1: The team produced 32 sketches. They grouped into five categories and evaluated all the sketches. Using the 20% rule, they each had six votes.

- Round 2: The team produced 10 sketches, but some sketches were almost identical. They reduced them down to six. Each person ranked their top two preferences. Most people had voted on two predominant sketches, so they decided to mash up.

In their mashup, the participants worked with these two sketches:

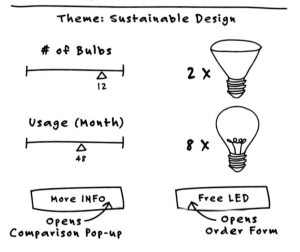

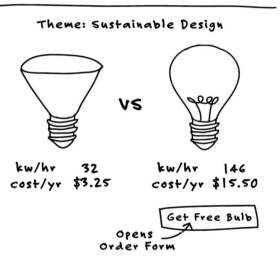

The mashup appears below:

MASHUP DESIGN

Brief description of LED and incandesent bulbs. User can get more
information to compare bulbs.

As someone moves the sliders the bulbs and numbers increase
and decrease.

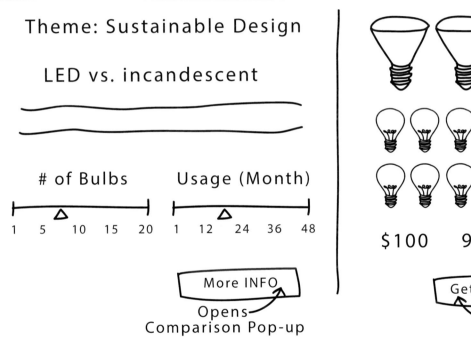

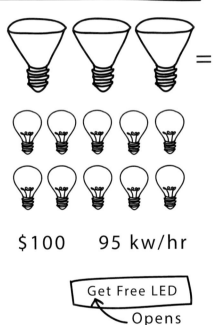

Tips and Tricks for Mashing Up

Based upon my experience, people are most successful with mashing up two or more ideas when they do the following things:

1. **Use a Whiteboard.** People change their mind during a mashup. It is inevitable. Use a large whiteboard with plenty of space. Make sure erasers are available.

2. **One Person Sketches.** When you have two or more people sketching, it is hard to follow. Use one person to sketch on the whiteboard, preferably not the Leader.

3. **Start with Containers.** Before you sketch too many details, you may want to start with the containers. You want everyone to agree on the location of design elements.

4. **Sketch Detailed Navigation.** After sketching containers, I recommend sketching your navigation, which helps people to know where they are and where they can go.

5. **Sketch the Default View First.** When a page has different states, draw the default view, because it will be what your customers initially see.

6. **Take a Picture When You Are Done.** You want to take a picture when you are done and everyone agrees to a common vision. Keep a digital copy for people to review.

7. **Sketch Additional Interactions, as Needed.** Tweak the sketch to show additional interactions (pop-ups, different views). Take a picture and store a digital copy for the new sketches, too.

8. **Send the Pictures to a Designer.** Lastly, the pictures from your mashup should be sent to a designer to render a high-fidelity mockup to be further reviewed by the team.

Summary

- Mashing up is the process of merging two or three ideas into a single concept.
- Mashing up differs from other sketching activities in two ways:
  - o It is a group activity rather than an individual sketching exercise.
  - o It is done on whiteboard rather than paper.
- The mashup is one of the last activities you do in a design studio.
- The mashup(s) will be given to a designer to create a high-fidelity mockup.
- Tips for a successful mashup:
  - o Use a whiteboard.
  - o One person sketches.
  - o Start with containers.
  - o Sketch detailed navigation.
  - o Sketch the default view first.
  - o Take a picture and store a digital copy after each mashup.
  - o Sketch additional interactions, as needed.
  - o Send the pictures to a designer to render a high-fidelity mockup.

CHAPTER 15

Presenting Your Mockups (or Selling Your Vision to Everyone)

When you finish a design studio, you have just started the first 10% of your project. Your participants are exhausted, but happy with their progress. Paper, markers, tape, rulers, sticky notes, and more are scattered around a cluttered room. Your work, however, is just beginning. You need to share your vision with everyone:

- **Product Team.** These people will build, test, market, sell, and support your vision.
- **Executives.** These decision-makers provide you with time, money, and resources.
- **Customers.** These people buy, upgrade, upsell, cancel, call support, and more.

In this chapter, you will learn how to interact with each of these very important stakeholders within the first few weeks of finishing your design studio.

"Art is making something out of nothing and selling it."
– Frank Zappa

STEP #9: Present Mockups

TIME, MONEY, RESOURCES

Getting Buy-In Through Participation

An easy way to get buy-in from customers, Executives, and a product team is to include them in your design studio. For me, the sense of ownership that design studio participants take by going through the process of generating and evaluating ideas gets them to buy into the final vision. Relationships are formed, along with designs. Discussions and decisions are remembered.

You should invite **influencers** to participate in your design studio. An influencer is accepted, connected, and respected by Executives, customers, and the product team. In some cases, these influencers may not be in leadership positions, but they hold a lot of power within an organization. Other people listen when an influencer speaks. While you may not be able to get a customer or Executive to participate, try to get an influencer who can participate and communicate with them.

YOUR BEST MARKETER IS A SKEPTIC TURNED TRUE BELIEVER

The best marketing comes from converting a skeptical person into a believer. On one project, I had an expert who did not want to listen to other perspectives. With over 20 years of experience, the expert was also an influencer with the product team, Executives, and customers. She had talked with customers, performed demos, launched products, and served this product community for longer than most people could remember. She was initially skeptical of the design studio method, so I stroked her ego.

My argument was simple: She was the expert and we needed her participation. Then, knowing her input was so valuable, this expert followed the design studio rules and used the different techniques. She loved the process and collaboration with other participants. She brought a wealth of experience, stories, and insights. She contributed at every opportunity. After the design studio, the skeptical expert had been converted to a true believer. She told everyone—Executives, customers, other teams, her spouse, their children, and anyone who would listen. Buy-in came through participation. She marketed the design studio method to the whole company.

Your best marketing comes from converting a skeptical person into a true believer.

You will have to sell your vision. You will not be able to pack all your customers, Executives, and product team members into your design studio. While these groups may not participate in generating and evaluating ideas in the design studio, you can have them contribute in other ways. The rest of this chapter describes ways to sell your vision to these other groups by including them in various activities.

Working with Your Product Team

After completing the design studio, you need to involve your product team to obtain their feedback and gain their support of your vision. While the design studio participants came up with an idea, your product team makes it a reality. As you develop an idea, it will change. You learn more about a solution when you actually produce it. Your idea will be reviewed by marketers, engineers, designers, writers, quality assurance people, managers, accountants, trainers, lawyers, and more. Each person brings a unique perspective.

You do not need to involve the entire product team right away. You should be strategic in how you approach different people. You have heard the old saying that "timing is everything" in business. The planning of "your timing" is critical to your success. In other words, you need to plan how to pitch your new idea(s) to the people who will implement it. The timing of the team's involvement occurs in very distinct intervals:

1. **Designing the Mockup.** Initially, you need a designer to build a high-fidelity mockup based on the final sketch. This person may need to consult with the Sketchers, since the designer may not have been a participant in the design studio.

2. **Refining Your Concept.** After the mockup is created, you want to show it to key influencers, managers, and subject matter experts. You want them to review for technical accuracy and completeness. Plus, you want to answer any questions.

TIP #2:

Do not involve the whole team right away. Be strategic.

3. **Getting Executive Support.** Do not approach Executives until your sketches have been rendered into high-fidelity mockups and reviewed by experts. Executives want to see the vision (high-fidelity mockup) and know experts have reviewed it.

4. **Gaining Broader Team Support.** Assume the idea gets approved by the Executives. Now, you need to gain support from the product team to develop it. At this point, you should consider a "road show" to explain the idea and get their support.

5. **Developing the Product.** As the product gets developed, you will need to stay in contact with different teams to ensure they are executing on your vision. The design will change based upon what people learn by developing an idea.

Again, timing is everything in business. Do not forget how to better plan the timing of your communication with Executive, product team, and customers.

TIP #3:

If timing is everything, you should plan "your timing" with the team.

Getting Executive Buy-In

The final sketch from a design studio is completely worthless without Executive buy-in. Executives make things happen. With their approval, you get the time, money, and resources you need to make a great idea turn into a reality. At some point, you will need to show a presentation to Executives to get their buy-in. All presentations to Executives should be credible, memorable, clear, concise, and emotional. Use pictures and stories to explain your design studio results. The length of your presentation will vary, but it should still be short.

For the sake of clarity, the next section will review a sample presentation. You can download this presentation from the companion website for this book: http://www.designstudiomethod.com.

TIP #4:

Your design studio is completely worthless without Executive buy-in.

Sample Presentation to Get Executive Buy-In

This presentation is based upon the light bulb widget created for World Usability Day. Beside each slide, you will see my speaker notes and the reason for presenting each one.

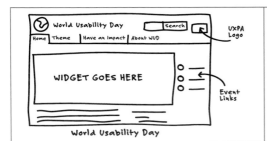

Speaker Notes:

Before we begin, I want to thank Elizabeth for allowing us to do this design studio. We will explain the process and show our final design.

Reasons:

You need to show respect and build rapport.

	Standard	LED
Bulb Power	50 watts	4.2 watts
Initial Price	$2.00	$42.50
KwH per Year	146	32
Yearly Operating Costs	$15.50	$3.25
Lifetime of Bulbs (Hours)	715	5000
Total Dollar Costs	$197.50	$85.00
Total Energy Used	250,000	21,000

Speaker Notes:

With a goal to create a widget to get people to switch to an LED bulb, we learned the energy and cost savings of standard and LED bulbs.

Reasons:

You need to build credibility and to show you did your research.

GENERATE IDEAS   EVALUATE IDEAS

1. Strive for Quantity
2. Defer Judgment
3. Seek New Combinations
4. Use Your Imagination

1. Use Positive Judgment
2. Consider Novelty
3. Narrow Deliberately
4. Stay on Course

BLUE WHITE GREEN   YELLOW BLACK RED

Speaker Notes:

We performed a design studio, which is a sketching workshop with several people. Participants followed specific rules to generate and evaluate the sketches. We used the Six Thinking Hats to help us reach our decision.

Reasons:

You may need to educate Executives. It builds credibility by explaining the process.

QA   MARKETING

DEV   UX

Speaker Notes:

Participants initially sketched alone to avoid groupthink and ensure individual creativity.

Reasons:

You are still educating and building credibility.

QA   DEV   UX   MARKETING

Speaker Notes:

Participants presented their sketches. Other participants critiqued the sketches for positive and negative aspects. They voted on the most intriguing and innovative ideas.

Reasons:

You are still educating and building credibility.

42

Speaker Notes:

Forty-two different concepts for the widget were generated and evaluated by participants.

Reasons:

You are building credibility for the group now.

+

Speaker Notes:

In the final round, two concepts were mashed up into a final design.

Reasons:

You are building credibility for the group now.

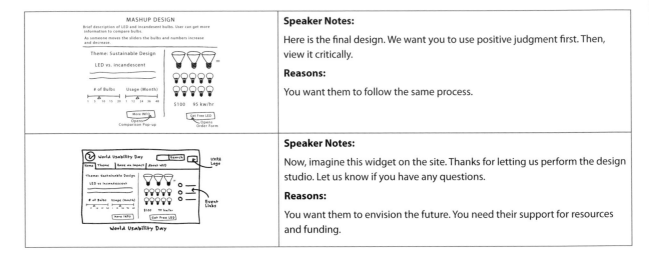

	Speaker Notes:
MASHUP DESIGN	Here is the final design. We want you to use positive judgment first. Then, view it critically.
	Reasons:
	You want them to follow the same process.
	Speaker Notes:
	Now, imagine this widget on the site. Thanks for letting us perform the design studio. Let us know if you have any questions.
	Reasons:
	You want them to envision the future. You need their support for resources and funding.

TIP #5:

Make an Executive presentation credible, clear, concise, and emotional.

In this presentation, we used only nine slides in our conversation with the Executive Director of World Usability Day, Elizabeth Rosenzweig. The final concept was approved within minutes.

Use the Executive Presentation with the Product Team

If your design gets approved, you can re-use the Executive presentation with the product team and your customers. As mentioned earlier, you need to get the support of the product team after the Executive approves your design direction. You can show the presentation at staff meetings, where you can gain alignment and support from the managers and key influencers within your company. You can even show this presentation to customers to let them know your product's direction.

TIP #6:

Re-use the Executive presentation with your product team and customers.

Selling Your Vision to Customers: Involve Them

The single best way to sell your vision to a customer is to include them in your product's development. Designers want their customers involved in the creative process. Customers will bring their own unique perspectives, aspirations, goals, desires, wants, and needs to your attention. You just need to involve them. It is a co-operative approach to design and customer engagement. It creates a very strong relationship built upon mutual respect and trust. When you involve your customers, your products are easier to sell.

TIP #7:

Sell the value of your new idea to customers by involving them in its design.

Let's assume your design studio was successful. An Executive gives you the time, money, and resources you need, and your product team fully supports the new design. At this point (maybe earlier), you should involve your customers in the design of your product. The following list provides some proven design and usability methods you can use to obtain customer feedback:

- **Contextual Interviews**. Talk with customers about how they perform tasks. You could show them your mockup at the end of the interview for additional feedback.

- **Card Sorting.** You may want to understand how your customers categorize information on your site or app. This method is a great way to understand navigation.

- **Task Analysis.** You work with your customers to understand all of the steps they go through to complete a task. You can see if your new design improves their task flow.

- **Design Walkthroughs**. Give your customers a basic task they might do using your mockup. See how they do. This method is useful to see your design's intuitiveness.

- **Rapid Iterative Testing Evaluations (RITE).** Customers test a design. You change the design, as needed. The same tasks get repeated on updated designs.

- **Baseline Usability Testing.** When development is finishing, perform a usability test to set a baseline for the product. You can identify and fix any last-minute issues.

- **Web Analytics.** After a product is released, web analytics allow you to see what customers are doing. You may need to tweak your design based on what you see.

- **User Surveys.** You can perform many different kinds of customer surveys, such as the SUMI (Software Usability Measurement Inventory) or SUS (System Usability Scale), to determine your product's acceptance and usability.

TIP #8:

You can prevent design and usability issues by involving your customers.

Summary

- You must sell your vision to the product team, Executives, and customers.
  - o Product teams turn your idea into a reality.
  - o Executives give you time, money, and resources.
  - o Customers buy, sell, trade, upgrade, cancel, and more.
- You should time the product team's involvement:
  - o Phase 1: A designer creates a high-fidelity mockup.
  - o Phase 2: Experts evaluate the high-fidelity mockup.
  - o Phase 3: Seek Executive buy-in for product vision, approval, and resources.
  - o Phase 4: Once approved, gain support of managers and influencers.
  - o Phase 5: Monitor the progress during development.
- When presenting to Executives, know these things:
  - o Executives empower your product team.
  - o Use pictures and stories in Executive presentations.
  - o Your slides should tell a story.
  - o Show the current state and the future state (your high-fidelity mockup).
  - o Make them use positive judgment first.
- Sell customers on your vision by:
  - o Including them in your product's design and development.
  - o Using a combination of many different methods (usability, RITE study, surveys).
  - o Monitoring their usage with web analytics after a product is released.
- Best Practices for Selling Your Vision include:
  - o Tip #1: Do not involve the whole team right away. Be strategic.
  - o Tip #2: If timing is everything, plan "your timing" with the team.
  - o Tip #3: Your design studio is completely worthless without Executive buy-in.
  - o Tip #4: Executive slides should be credible, clear, concise, and emotional.
  - o Tip #5: Re-use the Executive presentation with your product team and customers.
  - o Tip #6: Sell the value of your new idea to customers by involving them in its design.
  - o Tip #7: You can prevent design and usability issues by involving your customers.

PART 3
Advanced Topics

CHAPTER 16

Working Remotely with People

On most projects, I collaborate with several people in different geographic locations. Two years ago, I worked on a project where the team was literally scattered across the globe. We had 24 people in different roles in the following locations:

"Shoot. Move. Communicate."

- **United States (Dallas)**. Marketing and Usability were on the same campus.
- **Uruguay (Montevideo)**. Client Support sat on different floors of the same building.
- **Poland (Krakow).** Developers and Designers sat near each other in the same office.
- **Germany (Berlin).** Two Database Administrators shared a cubicle and one phone.
- **Russia (Moscow).** Our Moscow-based client serves its customers globally.

At the end of the project, we delivered a high-quality product that our Moscow-based client uses every day with its customers all over the world. In this chapter, you will learn how to collaborate with remote participants more effectively on your design studio projects.

Working Remotely with People

In the Marines, Sergeants tell their Lieutenants to remember three things to be a successful troop leader: shoot, move, and communicate. Sergeants know that the best leaders must think fast, make decisions, and speak clearly. In the context of a design studio, "shoot" means you target the best designs, analyze your options, and pick the best ones. When you "move" in a design studio, you adapt your sketches based upon what you learn—adding, modifying, deleting, and moving design elements to seek out new, innovative opportunities. Finally, design studio participants must "communicate" to inform, update, show, evaluate, and decide. On all your projects, you should shoot, move, and communicate.

Collaboration Strategies for Design Studios

"Amateurs talk about tactics, but professionals study logistics."
– General Robert H. Barrow, USMC

The success of any design studio project depends upon how well you handle logistics. Wars, businesses, and holidays succeed or fail because of logistics. Based upon my experience, you can do your design studio in three different ways:

- **Location-Based Approach.** Work with people in the same geographic location.

- **Travel-Based Approach.** Remote participants travel to one destination to work.

- **Remote Collaboration.** You include remote participants, using collaboration tools.

Let's review each of these approaches in greater detail below.

Using a Location-Based Strategy

A location-based strategy is easy to implement and manage. Since your participants already work in the same area, your logistics are super easy. Whether you work in the same city, on the same campus, or on the same floor, you can easily schedule a meeting with little, or no, travel costs. You schedule some time, find a room, and get to work. You may have already worked with some of the participants on other projects. If you have not worked with someone before, you can quickly establish a rapport with them because they might be your neighbors.

A location-based strategy has drawbacks that can impact your design studio project. By working with a small group of people in the same location, your perspectives may be too narrowly focused. Your participants may be too like-minded, as they may have shared values and similar experiences because they live and work in the same area. The biggest issue with a location-based strategy is the potential for groupthink, which is the tendency for people to value group harmony rather than frank, honest discussions. Because people work together, they may value group harmony because their next meeting or project could be with one of your design studio participants. Finally, you squander the opportunity for diversity on the team, lose diverse perspectives, and risk alienating your co-workers by excluding remote participants.

A location-based approach is my least preferred approach.

Using a Travel-Based Approach

The travel-based approach is my preferred way to do design studios. You give your product team a huge boost by including remote participants. You increase the likelihood of diverse thinking with the inclusion of people from different locations. Remote participants can focus solely on the design studio without the typical distractions of their daily workplace. From a team viewpoint, people can connect with each other, establish a rapport, and build trust. When remote participants leave, they will have a shared vision of your design direction. With this knowledge, they can help you get the product developed.

TIP #1:

You lose diverse viewpoints when you use a location-based approach.

TIP #2:

The best approach is a travel-based strategy, where people are in the same room.

PEOPLE TRAVEL TO ONE LOCATION

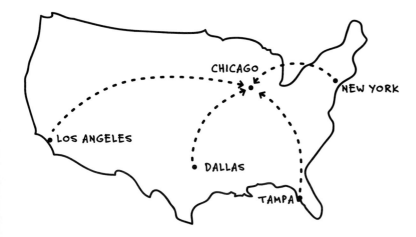

TIP #3:

When remote employees travel in for a design studio, they are more committed.

TIP #4:

Be a gracious host to build team camaraderie and focus your travelers.

While a travel-based strategy has many advantages, it has more logistical issues. Clearly, people must travel to a new location. During their trip, they may encounter a series of travel-related issues, such as jet lag, booking their travel, airport security, lost luggage, flight delays, language barriers, and more. For your design studios, scheduling becomes your primary logistical issue. You need to schedule enough time for remote participants to book their travel, do their sketches, drive to an unfamiliar location, and leave early enough to catch a return flight. During group collaboration, you will need to be flexible with remote participants. To account for jet lag, you can schedule your start time a little later on the first day. Schedule breaks to give remote participants an opportunity to call home or recover from jet lag. If you see people yawning, suggest a walk outside, stretching, or a coffee break. You can compensate for almost all of the logistical issues associated with remote people traveling to your location.

From my experience, getting remote participants to travel to a single location is better than using remote collaboration tools. You can more easily evaluate sketches in person. You can interpret someone's body language better in person than viewing it on a small screen with a web cam. You notice the inflection and sarcasm in a person's voice with face-to-face communication that does not come across in a telephone call. When you get participants in the same room, no technology is needed to collaborate. Participants show their sketches, critique them, and make decisions by talking to each other. You are better off using less technology to do creative problem-solving.

Using a Remote Collaboration Strategy

You may choose to include participants by using a remote collaboration strategy. In this approach, you include remote people by using different technology to allow for collaboration. During the initial meetings, you may use screen-sharing software and a conference line to show a presentation of the design studio process. The Product Manager may send an email with a document of business requirements attached. If a remote participant has a question, they can use their phone, chat, text, email, and more. While technology makes it easier to do remote collaboration, it has the most logistical considerations.

From a logistical viewpoint, remote participants will need to use technology for a variety of reasons. Luckily, most remote people will be familiar with these tools. Remote participants use collaboration tools for the following reasons:

- **Project Management.** This technology allows you to instantly communicate with collaborators. Everyone gets the same update and same file at the same time.

- **Conference Calling.** Conference calls allow for instant voice feedback. Unlike chat, people can immediately ask questions or provide answers.

Needs of Working Remotely

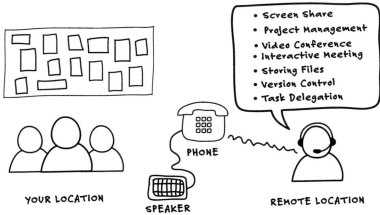

- **Screen Sharing.** Desktop sharing allows someone to see another person's screen. Use desktop sharing in design studios to evaluate sketches with remote people.
- **Video Conferencing.** These tools allow you to see and hear remote people. Body language can be read. People feel more connected.
- **Interactive Meetings.** With a shared online whiteboard, people add ideas, photos, or videos. They can organize, prioritize, comment, and vote on ideas in real time, too.
- **Storing and Updating Files.** Remote participants need access to a shared location to review or update the files later.
- **Version Control.** Use online version-control tools to track changes that happen within directories or files. These tools are useful when you tweak your wireframes.
- **Task Delegation.** As you move from ideation to development, you need to delegate tasks and create "to-do" lists with remote people to ensure that nobody duplicates work.
- **Social Communication.** Online social platforms allow for remote employees to engage in casual communications and create social groups with other employees.

Remote collaboration tools exist for almost any project need. Consider what you need from the remote participants, when you decide on your technology needs.

TIP #5:

Consider your communication needs when selecting remote collaboration tools.

A Side-by-Side Comparison

The following table shows a side-by-side comparison of the advantages and disadvantages with each approach.

	Location-Based	**Travel-Based**	**Remote Collaboration**
Advantages	• Same location • Easy to schedule • People know each other	• Includes remote people • Helps team to connect • Removes distractions	• Includes remote people • No travel required • More participation
Disadvantages	• Excludes remote people • Groupthink • Too narrowly focused	• Must pay travel costs • May be hard to schedule • Jet lag affects people	• Technology issues • More setup time • Time considerations

12 Tips for Working with Remote Participants

Follow these tips to successfully collaborate with remote participants in a design studio:

1. **Do Not Have a Remote Historian.** If the Leader and Historian are in different locations, it only adds confusion. These roles should be in the same location. These people need to work together as a team to lead the rest of the design studio group.

2. **Limit the Number of Remote Participants.** Group collaboration is easier when people are in the same room. If possible, limit the number of remote Sketchers to two people. You only increase logistical issues with more remote people.

3. **Define Roles and Responsibilities Early.** You have less access to remote people, so you must set expectations, define their roles, and describe their responsibilities. With a clear direction, remote participants will do their sketches.

4. **Ask Them to Turn Off Other Technology.** They should not chat, text, or surf the Internet during a design studio. You need their attention and focus. Remind them to respect other people's time. They should only use the pre-defined collaboration tools.

5. **Their Sketches Must Be Turned in Early.** Remote participants should turn in their sketches early, so their sketches can be printed and hung for

other people to review them. This rule provides peer pressure to other participants in the room, too.

6. **Ask (or Tell) Remote Participants to Use a Headset.** Remote participants may be tempted to use a speaker phone. Nobody wants to hear background noise. Everyone needs to hear their comments and questions. Ask (or tell) them to use a headset.

7. **Consider a Virtual Meeting on the Last Day.** After your participants reach consensus, consider a virtual meeting to recap the design studio. Video conferencing helps to build team chemistry and build further alignment on your design direction.

8. **Tell Remote Participants to Mute Their Phone.** You do not want unnecessary sounds on a conference line. Ask remote participants to mute their phone, so participants can hear what other people are saying. When they present or critique sketches, you may need to remind remote participants to take their phone off mute.

9. **Keep in Close Contact.** Periodically, check-in with remote participants. Make sure people know what to do. Identify their preferred remote communication tool. Schedule regular intervals to build your relationship with them.

10. **Do a Virtual Coffee Break.** To build team morale and establish camaraderie, do a virtual coffee break with remote participants. The best conversations can happen when two people informally meet to drink coffee.

11. **Be Respectful of Time.** When working with remote participants, you need to be respectful of time zones. You might need to adjust the start or end time of the design studio based upon a better time for remote participants.

12. **Ask for Trust, If Needed.** In some cases, you may have to ask remote participants to trust the participants in the room. For example, clustering of sketches and mashing up the final sketch is easier for participants in the same room. Ask for trust, if needed.

Summary

- Successful design studios are determined by how well you handle logistics.
- Three strategies to handle remote participants:
  - **Location-Based Only (least preferred).** You ignore remote participants.
  - **Travel-Based (most preferred).** Remote people travel to one location.
  - **Remote Collaboration.** You use collaboration tools with remote people.
- Use collaboration tools for these types of activities:
  - Project Management.
  - Conference Calling.
  - Screen Sharing.
  - Video Conferencing.
  - Interactive Meetings.
  - Storing Files.
  - Version Control.
  - Task Delegation.
  - Social Communication.
- Best Practices for working with remote participants:
  - Tip #1: Do not have a remote Historian.
  - Tip #2: Limit the number of remote participants.
  - Tip #3: Define roles and responsibilities early.
  - Tip #4: Ask them to turn off other technology.
  - Tip #5: Their sketches must be turned in early.
  - Tip #6: Ask them to use a headset.
  - Tip #7: Consider a virtual meeting on the last day.
  - Tip #8: Remind them to mute their phone, except when presenting or critiquing.
  - Tip #9: Keep in close contact to answer questions.
  - Tip #10: Take a virtual coffee break with remote participants.
  - Tip #11: Be respectful of time, especially their time zone.
  - Tip #12: Remote participants may need to trust the decisions of the people in one location. Ask for trust, if needed.

CHAPTER 17

Storing Your Work to Re-visit Later

I firmly believe that storing your work is so important that it needs its own chapter.

"Write well. Edit often."
– Susan Stratham

BANK LIKE BERLIN: SAVE AND RE-VISIT YOUR WORK

In 1918, Irving Berlin was writing songs for a military revue. When his assistant told him to cut a song, Berlin chose "God Bless America" because he was not satisfied with the lyrics. So, he stored the song in a trunk. Twenty years later, Irving Berlin changed just a few words:

Original lyric: "Stand beside her and guide her to the right with a light from above."

New lyric: "Stand beside her and guide her through the night with a light from above."

On November 11, 1938, Kate Smith sang "God Bless America" on her annual Armistice Day broadcast for the first time. "God Bless America" was an instant hit … 20 years later.

Thankfully, Irving Berlin saved and re-visited his work.

Storing your work is the most important and mundane task of a design studio.

Sketchers have spent their energy generating and evaluating ideas. After guiding the group, an exhausted Leader may be tempted to throw away the sketches. The Historian will be cleaning up the room, rearranging the furniture, downloading pictures, or talking with participants. Everyone may forget about the original sketches when the team has just mashed up the final vision on a whiteboard.

Throwing away a sketch is like throwing away an idea. Stop doing it. Now!

SAVE & RE-VISIT YOUR WORK

BANK LIKE BERLIN

Giving Hardcopy Sketches to the Product Manager

Your Product Manager should have all the hardcopy sketches. Use file folders to group the sketches together. Label the file folders using the same categories used by your participants. By having the Historian take pictures, you already have a digital copy to use as a back-up.

Product Managers can use these sketches to:

- Recall different conversations during the design studio.
- Review different designs that might be used later.
- Use the sketches on another project.
- Represent as visual notes from the design studio.
- Show in a presentation to other team members and executives.
- Hang around a collaboration area to inspire others.
- Re-visit previous ideas when another one does not work.

In my experience, Product Managers enthusiastically thank you for giving them the sketches.

TIP #1:

Always give your hardcopy sketches to the Product Manager.

GIVE SKETCHES TO PRODUCT MANAGER

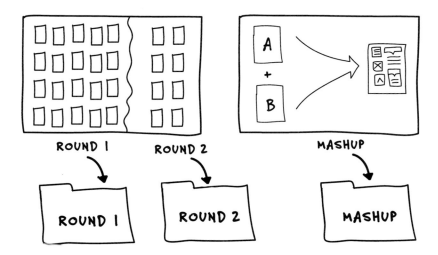

ROUND 1   ROUND 2   MASHUP

ROUND 1   ROUND 2   MASHUP

KEEPING A DIGITAL COPY OF ALL SKETCHES

You should store your sketches digitally. You can do many things with digital assets: search, zoom in, zoom out, copy, paste, email, and tag. The Historian will take photos of all of the sketches during the design studio. Store the photos in a location where all of the participants can access them from a work device.

Follow these best practices for storing your digital photos from a design studio:

- Always take photos of all the sketches and store them digitally.
- Set up a storage location before the Sketchers begin evaluating concepts.
- Use the same categories and labels used by your design studio participants.
- Provide a meaningful name to each of the photo files.
- If possible, tag the photos to make them easier to find when people search.
- Do not delete any files from a device until you know they are stored digitally.

TIP #2:

Create a storage location before people evaluate the sketches.

TIP #3:

The Historian takes and stores photos.

Sharing Your Digital Sketches with Other People

Use your best judgment on when and how to share access to your digital sketches. You may want to strategically delay access to the digital photos to allow the Designer to create a high-fidelity mockup. Plus, the Product

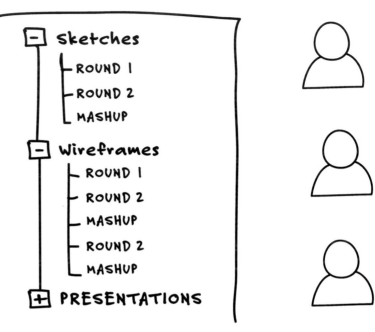

STORE DIGITAL COPIES

- [-] **Sketches**
  - ROUND 1
  - ROUND 2
  - MASHUP
- [-] **Wireframes**
  - ROUND 1
  - ROUND 2
  - MASHUP
  - ROUND 2
  - MASHUP
- [+] **PRESENTATIONS**

TIP #4:

Create a high-fidelity mockup and presentation before giving access to others.

Manager may want to create a presentation to show the larger team and Executives. Giving access to other people may invite unnecessary scrutiny before you are ready.

All participants from the design studio should have access immediately to the photos. Your Designer will need the final sketch to create a high-fidelity mockup. Other people can wait a few days until your work is done.

Re-visiting Previous Sketches

Over the past few years, I have been studying the habits of great designers and artists like Leonardo da Vinci, Saul Bass, Henri Matisse, Steve Jobs, and Pablo Picasso. These designers all re-visited their work. For example, Leonardo da Vinci produced over 13,000 pages of sketches in his lifetime. The *Codex Atlanticus* contains most of his military sketches, which were produced over a 20-year period. Da Vinci catalogued his sketches and grouped them together. You can design like da Vinci by re-visiting your work.

As described previously, Irving Berlin stored and re-visited "God Bless America" after 20 years. For Berlin, his wooden trunk provided him with a reserve to re-visit (and re-work) previous ideas. Today, you really have no excuse. Smartphones have cameras. Network speed makes downloading pictures very fast, too. Pinterest, Instagram, and Flickr offer quick ways to store photos. Think of the opportunities.

CREATE A VISION BOARD

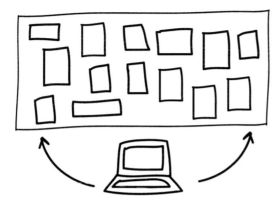

- PREVIOUS SKETCHES
- WIREFRAMES
- SCREEN SHOTS

- OTHER SITES
- PATTERNS
- COMPETITORS

- Do you review design pattern libraries?
- Do you store your ideas?
- Do you remember to re-visit previous ideas?
- What design artifacts do you keep?

Storing the photos from a design studio creates design artifacts for you and your team!

You should re-visit earlier sketches (or design artifacts) for discussions, spotting patterns, or inspiration. Several years ago, I was leading a design studio, where the primary goal was to create an executive dashboard of key performance indicators (KPIs) for a business unit. As it turns out, some participants misunderstood the instructions. Rather than sketch for Executives, some participants had sketched an operational dashboard for Account Directors. We saved our work and re-visited it six months later when we needed it.

Draw inspiration from your earlier sketches. After you have worked on several design studio projects, you will have a large set of design artifacts. You can include some earlier sketches into a vision board, which is a collection of pictures, words, and images to help inspire your imagination. Pinterest, Flickr, Evernote, or any shared location offer you low-cost ways to store your sketches and create vision boards.

TIP #5:

Use your earlier sketches to create a vision board for new projects.

DESIGN LIKE DA VINCI: THE BRIDGE THAT TOOK 500 YEARS TO CREATE

In 1502, the Sultan of Istanbul wanted to build a bridge over the Golden Horn Bay. The bridge would open up commerce to the northern lands and serve as a lookout tower for his navy. In search of a patron, Leonardo da Vinci would place a bid for this project by producing a sketch detailing many of the unique features of the bridge.

The Sultan gave da Vinci's sketch to his engineers, who rejected it. According to the Sultan's engineers, the bridge was too high and the support system would not work. Da Vinci was embarrassed. He stored the sketch of the Golden Horn Bay bridge with thousands of other sketches.

In 1991, the Leonardo da Vinci Bridge was built in Norway. The Sultan's engineers were completely wrong. It worked perfectly! Da Vinci's unique bridge specifications were simply ahead of their time. Thankfully, da Vinci stored his sketch. More importantly, it was Vebjørn Sand, a Norwegian artist, who re-visited the sketch of the Golden Horn Bay and oversaw its construction.

Summary

- Storing your work is the most important and mundane task of a design studio.

- Use the same categories and labels used in the design studio when storing the work.

- Always store the photos digitally on a shared drive.

- Use your best judgment when sharing with others.

- Re-visit previous sketches that you have saved.

- Best Practices include:

  o Tip #1: Give your hardcopy sketches to your Product Manager.

  o Tip #2: Create a storage location before people evaluate the sketches.

  o Tip #3: The Historian takes photos and stores them.

  o Tip #4: Create your high-fidelity mockup and presentation before giving access to others.

  o Tip #5: Use your earlier sketches to create a vision board for new projects.

CHAPTER 18

Next Steps

When your design studio ends, the real work begins. The design studio is really just the first of many steps in a product's development. The final sketches represent many things:

"The journey of a thousand miles begins with one step."

– Lao Tzu

1. **Product Alignment.** The final designs mean the team has alignment based upon the sketches that were created and evaluated. Since you did not have to sit in meeting after meeting with circular conversations, you quickly get alignment by doing the visual thinking of a design studio.

2. **Focused Direction.** The final sketches from a design studio represent a focused direction (or vision) for the team. You can share this vision almost immediately. Based upon my experience, you can see 75% of the final designs in the finished product. The design studio gets the product team solving the same problem.

3. **Starting Point for Future Discussions.** Your final sketches are the starting point of future discussions. Designers look at the sketches to create polished mockups or prototypes. You can show them to Executives to get buy-in. Usability testing can be done on your sketches with customers. Your final sketches start many conversations.

While a design studio provides a design strategy, vision, and direction, it is just your first step. In this chapter, let's review your next steps to ensure the execution of these ideas.

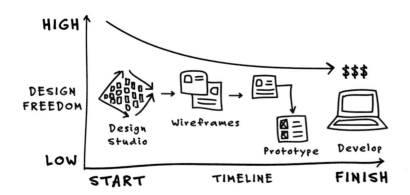

Things to Do Before People Leave the Room

Before your people leave the room, your next steps begin. Design studios are mentally exhausting. People must think, sketch, group, evaluate, vote, re-sketch, critique, order, and more. Within a very short timeframe, you place a large mental load on people, who already must balance their busy home and work lives. In addition, some people may have traveled from a different city (or country) to participate in the design studio. They will be physically exhausted. When your design studio ends, make sure you do a **Design Studio Debrief** to set expectations, thank participants, assign deliverables, and outline all of the next steps. It is a critical first step!

Use the following checklist for debriefing design studio participants before they leave the room:

- Thank everyone for their participation, ideas, and collaboration.
- Tell participants how many sketches were done in the design studio.
- Explain how a Designer will create mockups of the final sketches.
- Let participants know that they may be contacted for additional feedback.
- Advise participants that they will review mockups created by the Designer.
- Set expectations, timelines, and deliverables with a Designer.
- Explain how participants can review the sketches online (include the location of the images).
- Take a picture of all the participants to share with them (builds camaraderie).
- Verify the Historian has saved the pictures (sketches, action shots, and team photo).
- Let them know a presentation will get created to show to Executives.
- Tell everyone to have safe trips, wherever their destinations might be.

"Lost time is never found again."
– Benjamin Franklin

Things to Do Within the First Week

Within one week, participants will begin to forget your design studio. They will have slept, traveled home, cleared out their email, met with their co-workers, and resumed their schedule with all of the daily habits they have developed. The details of the design studio rapidly begin to fade. Their short-term memory empties and fills with other details, moments, feelings, conversations, and more. Life goes on.

During these initial days, you want to stay engaged with your participants for many reasons. First, you want them to provide you with feedback, so you can further refine your own style. Second, you have many other tasks to do with your participants to ensure the successful implementation of your final solutions. Third, you want to keep the momentum started with your design studio. Lastly, it is easy to relax during the first few days after a design studio. Based upon my experience, the first 100 hours after a design studio are crucial for your long-term success.

REACT LIKE ROOSEVELT: GETTING OFF TO A GREAT START

Franklin D. Roosevelt pioneered the 100-day concept to measure his effectiveness while implementing the New Deal in 1933. The underlying truth of the 100-day concept is that U.S. presidents have their biggest opportunities for success when they first take office. They have just won an election or re-election. Their leadership style is either new or reinforced by their presidential victory. President Roosevelt worked with Congress to get 15 major bills passed within his first 100 days. Since Roosevelt established the 100-day concept, all U.S. presidents measure their effectiveness using it.

Similar to a President's first 100 days, you significantly improve your chance of adoption, acceptance, and approval within the first 100 hours of completing your design studio. Sketches get turned into mockups. These mockups get reviewed by participants and a Designer refreshes right away. The Product Manager builds slides to showcase the mockups to Executives. The Executive Meeting occurs within four to five business days of your design studio. You build so much project momentum within the first 100 hours by creating an infectious atmosphere of optimism. You should react like Roosevelt, but within the first 100 hours.

Use this timeline to consider what to do within the first 100 hours after a design studio:

Role	Monday	Tuesday	Wednesday	Thursday	Friday
Designer	Creates mockups to be reviewed.	Sends mockups to Sketchers.	Creates more mockups.	Revises mockups based on feedback.	
Product Manager	Creates slides for Executives.	Reminds people to turn in their reviews.	Schedules Executive Meeting.	Finalizes presentation.	Presents to the Executives.
Sketcher		Reviews mockups.	Sends revisions to Designer.	Sends revisions to Designer.	
Executive					Listens. Asks questions. Funds the work.

Ways to Involve Customers

Once your project is approved, involve your customers to get their feedback. As you continue to refine your ideas, you can involve your customers in many ways:

- **Customer Councils.** You can show the mockups at a Customer Council to get their initial feedback on your design direction. Make sure to let them know that these designs will continue to be refined.

- **Contextual Interviews.** When you visit your customer, ask them questions to get a better understanding of how they work. Show them the mockups towards the end of the interview. You may get additional insights based on your interview.

- **Design Inspection.** You can have design or usability experts review your mockups based upon a set of guidelines and best practices. You will receive recommendations to help improve your designs, which can be very detailed.

- **Design Walkthrough.** You can walk your customers through your mockups to see how they react. Do they accept the ideas? Do they know where to go? Is anything missing? Would they move anything around? Would they use it?

- **Five-Second Blink Test.** You can quickly determine what items resonate by showing your customers a page and taking it away after five seconds. These tests are fun and interactive, but they are also revealing. Online software is available, too.

- **RITE Study.** In the RITE (or Rapid Iterative Testing Evaluation) method, you ask customers questions about a design. Based upon their feedback, you make changes to the design. You perform the same test with a new design and new customers.

- **Baseline Usability.** When you get working software, you should get a baseline of your product's usability with your customers. You may be able to fix some things before it is released. Plus, you can prioritize known issues to fix in the future.

- **Analytics.** You want to know what customers do with your product when it is released. Analytics let you know where they go, how long they stay, when they abandon, and more.

The above list is not comprehensive. You can always pick up the phone to call a customer, especially when you have a sketch, mockup, prototype, or product to show them.

Things to Do After Reading This Book

1. Find a project suitable for a design studio. Or, make one up to practice.
2. Assemble a team.
3. Stick to the processes outlined in this book.
4. Review the appropriate chapter when you get stuck.
5. Have fun with design studios.

Ready, set, sketch, re-sketch, mashup!!!

Summary

- Do a Design Studio Debrief before participants leave on the last day.
- Your first 100 hours are critical:
    - o Product Managers must schedule a review with Executives.
    - o Designers must create mockups.
    - o Sketchers must review them.
    - o Product Managers must create slides for the Executives.
    - o Designers must revise mockups based on the Sketchers' feedback.
    - o Product Managers put the revised sketches in the slides for Executives.
    - o The slides are presented to Executives.
- You can engage your customers in many ways:
    - o Customer Councils.
    - o Contextual Interviews.
    - o Design Walkthroughs.
    - o Design Inspections.
    - o Five-Second Blink Tests.
    - o RITE Studies.
    - o Baseline Usability Tests.
    - o Analytics.

Index

References to illustrations are indicated in *italics*.